How To Listen To God

Charles Stanley

OLIVER
NELSON

Thomas Nelson Publishers
Nashville • Atlanta • London • Vancouver

Published in Nashville, Tennessee, by Thomas Nelson, Inc., Publishers, and distributed by Word Communications, Ltd., Richmond, British Columbia.

Scripture quotations are from the NEW KING JAMES VERSION. Copyright © 1979, 1980, 1982, Thomas Nelson, Inc., Publishers.

Scripture quotations marked NASB are from the New American Standard Bible © The Lockman Foundation 1960, 1962, 1963, 1968, 1971, 1972, 1973, 1975, 1977, and are used by permission.

Scripture quotations marked AMPLIFIED are from The Amplified New Testament, © 1954, 1958 by the Lockman Foundation (used by permission).

Scripture quotations marked KJV are from the King James Version of the Bible.

Printed in the United States of America.

A CROSSINGS BOOK CLUB EDITION

ISBN 0-8407-9041-4

To my grandfather,
George Washington Stanley,
who taught me early in life
how to listen to God.

Contents

CHAPTER ONE

Is God Still Talking?

PSALM 81 IS a sad saga of a people who would not listen
to God. The compassionate heart of the Father in His numerous attempts to gain Israel's attention and devotion
and their persistent rejection are revealed in verses 8-14:

> "Hear, O My people,
>   and I will admonish you!
> O Israel, if you will listen to Me!
> There shall be no foreign god among
>   you;
> Nor shall you worship any foreign god.
> I am the LORD your God,
> Who brought you out of the land of
>   Egypt;
> Open your mouth wide,
>   and I will fill it.
>
> "But My people would not heed My
>   voice,
> And Israel would have none of Me.
> So I gave them over to their own stubborn heart,
> To walk in their own counsels.
>
> "Oh, that My people would listen to
>   Me,
> That Israel would walk in My ways!

> I would soon subdue their enemies,
> And turn My hand against their
>   adversaries."

One can feel the pulsebeat of God as He pleads for the nation of Israel, saying, "Please listen to Me. Please hear My voice." Each of us, too, should ask, "Lord, have You been trying to tell me something that I desperately need to hear? Are You exhorting me to listen to Your Voice?" I wonder how many times God has spoken to us and we were not listening. I wonder how many times He had something specific we needed to hear, but we were too occupied to pay attention.

There was a time in my ministry when I was too occupied doing the Lord's work to pay attention to God's Voice. I was preaching six times a week, taping two television programs, traveling across the country, writing a book, pastoring the church, and administrating a large church staff and broadcast ministry (among other daily duties). As a result of all this activity, I found myself in the hospital for a week and out of circulation for three months. As I look back over that time, I realize that God was trying to get my attention through my body, but I didn't listen. Then, finally, I couldn't go any further.

I believe one of the most valuable lessons we can ever learn is how to listen to God. In the midst of our complex and hectic lives, nothing is more urgent, nothing more necessary, nothing more rewarding than hearing what God has to say. And, the Bible is explicit, God speaks to us just as powerfully today as in the days in which the Bible was written. His Voice waits to be heard, and having heard it, we are launched into the greatest, most exciting adventure we could ever imagine.

WHY GOD SPEAKS TODAY

We might ask, "Why would God still want to talk to us today? Hasn't He said enough from Genesis to Revelation?" There are several compelling reasons why God still has His lines of communication open with His people.

First and foremost, He loves us just as much as He loved the people of Old and New Testament days. He desires to fellowship with us just as much as He fellowshipped with them. If our relationship with Him is a one-way trip and there is no communication or dialogue between us and the Lord Jesus Christ, then there isn't much fellowship. Fellowship is nil when one person does all the talking and the other does all the listening. God still speaks to us today because He wants to develop a love relationship that involves a two-party conversation.

The second reason God still speaks today is that we need His definite and deliberate direction for our lives, as did Joshua, Moses, Jacob, or Noah. As His children, we need His counsel for effective decision making. Since He wants us to make the right choices, He is still responsible for providing accurate data, and that comes through His speaking to us.

A third reason God speaks today is that He knows we need the comfort and assurance just as much as did the believers of old. We have Red Sea experiences, when our backs are to the wall and we do not know which way to turn. We undergo failures just as Joshua and the people of Israel did at Ai. When we undergo such defeats, God knows our need for His assurance and confidence.

I believe *the most important reason God is still talking today is that He wants us to know Him.* If God has stopped talking, then I doubt we will ever discover what He is really like. If the priority of all of our goals is to know God, then there must be more than just a one-way trip. Rather, there must be a communication link in which He talks to us and we listen or we talk to Him and He listens.

HOW GOD SPOKE IN OLD AND NEW TESTAMENT DAYS

If God is still talking, how does He speak? We can discover His methods by reviewing the different ways He revealed Himself in Old and New Testament days. *First, He spoke by direct revelation.* By His Spirit He spoke to the spirit of men like Abraham, who one day heard God directly tell him to leave the land in which he was living and go into a land that God would show him:

> Now the LORD said to
> Abram:
> "Get our of your country,
> From your family
> And from your father's house,
> To a land that I will show you.
> I will make you a great nation;
> I will bless you
> And make your name great;
> And you shall be a blessing.
> I will bless those who bless you,
> And I will curse him who curses you;
> And in you all the families
>   of the earth shall be blessed" (Gen. 12:1,2).

Second, the Bible says God spoke through dreams. A good example is evident in the experiences of Daniel, to whom God revealed His world destiny in a series of dreams. Through visions Daniel saw the empires that were to come. In this way, God gave Daniel tremendous insight into future world events that are still in the process of unfolding today.

This is a point, however, in which we must be extremely careful. The Bible does not ever say to seek the mind of God in dreams. For instance, I remember one Saturday night when I dreamed that nobody was in church the next morning, except me. If I had adhered to that dream, I probably would have just stayed home and slept!

Neither are we ever encouraged in the Word of God to seek the mind of God through visions. I had a friend who was flying home from a business trip one day, when he saw the sun reflecting through the clouds making the form of a cross. He interpreted that vision to mean that he was saved. Unfortunately, that does not have anything to do with confession, repentance, or belief in the Lord Jesus Christ as the Bible explains salvation.

The only time God has used a vision or a dream speaking in my life was after I spent several weeks fasting and seeking to know the mind of the Lord. I had been rather restless in my spirit and knew God was up to something, but I didn't know exactly what. Then one night, out of desperation I cried out to God, asking Him to reveal His purpose. God replied quickly and bluntly, "I am going to move you." I said, "When?" In a split second the word *September* flashed across my mind, and immediately my burden was lifted. The stirring in my spirit was gone. I had nothing more to pray about. That September I moved from Florida to Atlanta. God revealed Himself, not because I was seeking a vision or a dream, but because I was seeking His mind. It was a vision, nevertheless, and something God used to convince me He was involved in the business at hand.

Third, God spoke through His written words, such as when He gave Moses the Ten Commandments and then used the Law to communicate to His people. God also spoke *audibly* in biblical days. Saul of Tarsus was on his way to persecute believers in Damascus. The Bible says that he "fell to the ground and heard a voice saying to him, 'Saul, Saul, why are you persecuting Me?' " (Acts 9:4).

Fourth, God spoke through His prophets. The prophets exclaimed, "Thus saith the Lord," and the people obeyed because they knew it came directly from God.

Fifth, God spoke through circumstances. We've all heard the story of how God revealed Himself to Gideon. God wanted Gideon to lead the nation of Israel in battle against the enemy. Being a little fearful, Gideon decided to lay out a fleece. In fact, he laid it out twice. One morning he asked that it be soaking wet in the midst of dry grass, and the next morning he asked that it be as dry as gunpowder in the midst of wet grass. God graciously reached down to Gideon and gave him the assurance and confidence he needed.

Sixth, He spoke through angels, introducing to Mary and Joseph the birth of Jesus Christ through angelic proclamation. *Seventh, God often spoke through the Holy Spirit.* You remember that in the life of Paul, who was on his way to Asia, God spoke to him through the Holy Spirit, forbidding him to go there: "Now when they had gone through Phrygia and the region of Galatia, they were forbidden by the Holy Spirit to preach the word in Asia. After they had come to Mysia, they tried to go into Bithynia, but the Spirit did not permit them" (Acts 16:6–7).

HOW GOD SPEAKS TODAY

While we marvel at the methods God used to speak to His chosen ones of old, our spirits long to engage in direct and meaningful communication in this present age. We want to proclaim along with the Samaritans' response to the woman at the well in John 4:42, "Now we believe, not because of what you said, for we have heard for ourselves and know that this is indeed the Christ, the Savior of the world."

We can be thankful that God is still in the communication business. He employs four principal methods of revealing Himself to the contemporary believer.

The Word of God

The Lord's primary way of speaking to us today is through His Word. We already have the complete revelation of God. He doesn't need to add anything else to this Book. The revelation of God is the unfolding truth of God by God about Himself. It is the inspiration of the Holy Spirit, controlling the minds of men who penned the pages that make up the Bible. The Bible is the breath of God breathed upon those men that they might know the truth.

Yes, the most assured way we can know we hear from God is through His Word. When we face difficulties and heartaches, rather than seek this counsel or that counsel, we should first go to the Scriptures.

God's Word was written to the people addressed in Scripture. Isaiah wrote to Judah, Paul wrote to the Corinthians, but the Scriptures were also written for us. The Bible is God's instruction book for His people.

The Lord spoke to Joshua and said:

"Only be strong and very courageous, that you may observe to do according to all the law which Moses My servant commanded you; do not turn from it to the right hand
or to the left, that you may prosper wherever you go. This
Book of the Law shall not depart from your mouth, but
you shall meditate in it day and night, that you may observe to do according to all that is written in it. For then
you will make your way prosperous, and then you will
have good success" (Josh. 1:7–8).

The book of the Law was Joshua's guide, his instruction
book in godly living. So the Bible is for us today.

How does this work out in a practical way for twenti-
eth-century believers? When we pray and seek guidance
about a decision, we should ask God to speak to us
through His Word and give us some advice to clarify our
direction. As we meditate upon the Word with our request or decision in mind, God will often lead us to an incident in Scripture, a passage, or even a single verse that
will relate to what concerns us. It may deal with our specific experience, or the principle governing our decision
may be prominent in the text.

Sometimes God will lead us to the source, to the same
passage over and over again. It is not that we choose to re-
read the same passage, but somehow we just seem to
continue to open the book to that text. On an occasion
when I was seeking the Lord's will about a decision I
faced, every morning for about three weeks I found myself reading Isaiah 6. I was into the third week before I realized that I was being rebellious toward the Lord with
regard to what He required of me. Somehow, He would
not let me escape those words in verse 8: "Also I heard
the voice of the LORD, saying, 'Whom shall I send, And
who will go for Us?' Then I said, 'Here am I! Send me.' "
When I finally said yes to the Lord, Isaiah 6 was no longer

prominent in my morning meditation.

Through His Word He directs us, challenges us, warns us, comforts us, assures us. I have found it to be one of the most rewarding experiences in my Christian life: to face a challenge and meditate upon the Word until I know He has spoken.

The Holy Spirit

A second method God uses to speak to us today is through the Holy Spirit. In fact the primary way Jesus spoke in the New Testament was through the Holy Spirit. Today, God still speaks to our spirits through His Spirit who now lives, dwells, and abides in us.

If we walk in the Spirit daily, surrendered to His power, we have the right to expect anything we need to hear from God. The Holy Spirit living within us and speaking to us ought to be the natural, normal life-style of believers. We can claim His presence, direction, and guidance.

Some years ago our church was in the process of purchasing a piece of property. I was really seeking the Lord. We were going to see the owner of the property, and the morning we were to meet, I was reading the Scriptures, and I came upon this particular verse:

> Your way, O God, is in the sanctuary;
> Who is so great a God as our God?
> You are the God who does wonders;
> You have declared Your strength
>   among the peoples (Ps. 77:13–14).

Well, that was all I needed to hear. In the course of conversation with the owner, he asked, "How much are you willing to pay for the property?" The Spirit of God immediately spoke to me and said, "Don't answer that."

So I didn't answer. I kept quiet. He kept on talking. I

never said a word. Finally, he said, "How about this price?" and named a figure. It was a fair one, and I accepted. God's Spirit spoke to me very clearly and distinctly, giving me the proper direction I needed. I feel that the outcome was one that pleased God and made His work effective. I believe that the Word of God and the Holy Spirit are God's two primary modes for speaking to believers today. When I say the Holy Spirit "speaks," I do not mean audibly. Rather, He impresses His will in my spirit or mind, and I hear Him in my inner being. Though not audible, the communication is precise nevertheless.

Other People

A third way God speaks to us is through other people. This became clear to me during a prolonged illness.

One Sunday I became very ill and had to go to the hospital. All I could do was sleep the first two days. On the third day, my wife came to visit, and we began talking, because God had impressed upon my heart the need to go back to the very beginning of my life and review it up to the present point. I felt He had something to show me, and I needed my wife to help me see it.

Every afternoon we talked. We talked the rest of that week, and all of the next week, and all of the next week. For three weeks she wrote and she listened. Toward the end of the third week, my wife looked over a mountain of paper where she had recorded the conversations and said, "I believe God has shown me what the problem is." When she told me, the problem in my life became clear to me for the first time. God absolutely spoke through my wife and showed me something that brought about one of the most dramatic changes in my ministry. Had I not listened, I would have missed a magnificent blessing.

Actually, the people we ought to listen to the most are those we live with every day. Those people who love us the most, those who pray for us the most, are often the instruments God uses to reveal Himself to us. I can name several people who, in a passing conversation, have said something that has altered the course of my life to some degree. Just a simple word in passing, just a word here or there from someone close to us (or on rare occasions from a casual acquaintance), can have dramatic consequences.

That is why we need to be very careful about what we say. Recognizing that we can be used as God's spokespersons should cause us to soberly examine our dialogue. Perhaps God has a message for the listener that he has chosen us to deliver, and our talking about the weather or a football game would detract from that message. Thus, we should seek to be alert, sensitive, and available to God's Voice.

Circumstances

A fourth way God speaks to us is through circumstances. I believe those weeks in the hospital were engineered by God so that I could hear what He was saying. Such circumstances take on many forms. Sometimes it is a failure. Sometimes it is a success. Sometimes it is a disappointment. Sometimes it is a tragedy, but God uses all circumstances in life to speak to us.

When I was a pastor in the Midwest, I witnessed to a particular man for a number of months, but he seemed uninterested. One afternoon, a policeman I knew called and asked me to ride with him to a home where there had been some sort of trouble. When we arrived, I recognized the house as the residence of the individual with whom I had been sharing Christ. As we approached the house, the policeman prepared me for what we would soon see saying, "You are not going to like what you see, but I need you to help me." Inside was a twelve-year-old boy lying in a pool of blood. He had taken a twelve gauge shotgun, used a clothes hanger to trigger it, held it up against his heart, and killed himself. He left a note to his parents, which read, "Dear Mom and Dad, I love you. I do not know whether I will go to heaven or hell. I am going to kill myself and find out." I was present when the father walked into the home. When we told him what had happened, his first reply was "Oh, my God." In a couple of weeks, he came to our church and trusted Jesus Christ as his personal Savior—but it cost him the life of his son.

So, today, God speaks to us in four primary ways. First, *through His Word*; second, *through the Holy Spirit*; third, *through other godly people*; and fourth, *through circumstances*. Now that we recognize that God still actively participates in communicating His message to believers today, we must endeavor to hear intently. When God speaks (and He does), everyone should listen. As David declared in Psalm 85:8, "I will hear what God the LORD will speak."

CHAPTER TWO

God's Goal in Communicating

GOD NEVER SAYS anything unless it is important and worth remembering. He doesn't engage in chitchat. He doesn't preface His remarks with anything. God is always to the point. He has something to say, and He says it precisely and concisely.

God speaks clearly because He has specific objectives in mind. Thus it is to our great benefit to know His goal in speaking to us. During my ministry, I have seen that God's purposes in communication seem to fall into three primary areas.

COMPREHEND THE TRUTH

When God speaks to us, *His first goal is that we may comprehend the truth.* He desires that we understand fully what He is saying. If the only language we speak is English, God isn't going to communicate in Hebrew, Russian, or Chinese. When God's speaking Voice seems indistinct at times, it is not because of His lack of clarity;

it is because there is usually something in our lives hindering a clear hearing of His Voice.

God has given to all believers a divine Person who lives within us to help us receive and understand the truth. God said in 1 Corinthians 2:9, through Paul: "Eye has not seen, nor ear heard, Nor have entered into the heart of man The things which God has prepared for those who love Him." At first glance, that seems incomprehensible. Then Paul explained by adding verse 10, "But God has revealed them to us through His Spirit. For the Spirit searches all things, yes, the deep things of God."

Thus all believers have within them the Holy Spirit who perfectly knows the mind of God and who receives and communicates to our spirits the truth God wants us to hear. Although we were born with a bent away from God, the moment we received Christ as our Savior, the Holy Spirit came in to teach us the truth of who God is.

Paul clearly stated this when he declared in 1 Corinthians 2:12, "Now we have received not the spirit of the world, but the Spirit who is from God, that we might know the things that have been freely given to us by God." The Greek word for "know" is *oido*, which means "fulness of knowledge." The person who does not have the Holy Spirit cannot understand the spiritual things of life because of a fallen nature (see 1 Cor. 2:14). Given over to a self-life, the unbeliever is absolutely incapable of understanding the things of God.

I believe God has three primary areas He wants us to comprehend. *First of all, under the heading of truth, He wants us to know the truth about Himself.* He wants us to not just talk about but to grasp His majesty, His holiness, His power, His love, His grace, and His joy. When we begin to comprehend these mighty truths about the person of God, our lives are enriched, enabled, and energized.

The apostle Paul's life was one tribulation after another; he was stoned, beaten, shipwrecked, slandered, rejected, imprisoned, and generally treated rather shabbily. Yet, in the midst of a life-style that few would term encouraging, Paul wrote his ultimate aim in life was to "know God." And surely he did. Even today, almost two thousand years later, can we think of an individual who has experienced a richer life?

Paul's life was enriched with the knowledge of God. He knew Jesus as the Deliverer from a Philippian jail, as Comforter in his incarceration, as Forgiver of his shameful past, as Healer on the Isle of Malta, as Guide in his missionary journeys. Paul comprehended the truth of the character and person of Jesus Christ, pressing on to know Him at all costs.

Second, God wants us to know the truth about ourselves. God wants us to realize our importance in the scheme of His eternal plans and that our peculiarities sometimes hinder us. But most of all, God wants us to know our position and our supernatural privileges of who we are in Christ.

For too many believers, our position in Christ is a little-known truth. Once we were born again by God's Spirit, His Spirit came to permanently indwell us, and His sovereign love placed us in Christ. "But of Him you are in Christ Jesus" (1 Cor. 1:30).

Since we are one with Christ, all His divine privileges become ours. His righteousness is ours because He abides in us and we in Him. His wisdom and His sanctification we can now appropriate as our own.

Just as a college diploma confers "all the honors and

privileges appertaining thereto," so our enrollment in the Lamb's Book of Life carries with it all the glorious distinctions of our new status as God's children with one big difference—we did not earn our position; it is a gift of grace from God.

Third, He wants us to know the truth about other people. God wants us to see them no longer in the light of earthly wisdom, but to view them as His chosen instruments and His creations.

An example of this occurred when I was going through a period of painful suffering in my personal life. God was sifting me, sanding me, pruning me, until I thought there would not be anything left. A friend who was one of my staff members (and remains so today) helped pull me through this valley.

In the most unforgettable fashion, he demonstrated unconditional love. Sometimes I was harsh, even rude and unkind, as I battled with myself and let it spill out on him. He never reacted. He would just say to me, "I understand. What can I do to help?" He never rejected me nor showed disappointment; he never admonished me in a threatening fashion. No matter what I shared (and I poured out my insides to him), he just loved me. Anytime I called upon him, he was there. He wept with me, prayed with me, laughed with me, and patiently listened to me. I always felt I had his full attention. Through his unwavering love we developed an unbreakable bond of deep-level friendship that strengthened my own intimacy with God.

When we begin to understand the truth of who God is and have a better understanding of ourselves as well as others, we are thoroughly equipped to be fruitful, productive servants on earth.

PASSIVE LISTENING VERSUS
AGGRESSIVE LISTENING

There are two kinds of listeners: *passive* and *aggressive*. A passive listener does not come to God to hear a decision from Him. The aggressive listener comes knowing and seeking to hear diligently what God has to say. If he is in church, his Bible is open and his pen is ready. If he participates in a Bible study, he is all ears and his mind is inquisitive. If he is involved in personal devotion, his notebook is replete with insight into God's ways. An involved listener is always probing, searching, and comparing what he hears with previous data he has accumulated. He wants to be sensitive to what God is saying; he thinks constantly, *How can I apply this to my life?* The aggressive listener is accurately depicted in Acts 17:11 where Paul spoke of the Berean Christians, saying, "These [Bereans] were more fair-minded than those in Thessalonica, in that they received the word with all readiness, and searched the Scriptures daily to find out whether these things were so." They weren't just saying, "Oh, Paul is coming." They were investigating the Word.

James said, "But the one who looks intently at the perfect law, the law of liberty, and abides by it, not having become a forgetful hearer but an effectual doer, this man shall be blessed in what he does" (1:25 NASB). Notice the word *intently.* That means that we are to listen and hear the Word of God with a fervent focus. We are not to sit idly and allow the Word of God to stay simply on the surface level.

One of the problems today in the body of Christ is that too many Christians have been passive listeners for too many years. That is why after forty years as believers, they won't teach a Bible study or lead a class because they "don't know the Word well enough." Where have they been for the past four decades?

We come to church, watch television, read, listen to radio, or attend revivals, seminars, or conferences so that we might listen to God, not man. Man doesn't have much to say, but when God is speaking through His servants, then the hearer must aggressively hear what God is imparting. The passive listener comes into a church service or Bible study and never gives a second thought to what God is speaking. He is not involved in the hearing process. If God were to send Charles Stanley a letter and address it, DEAR CHARLES, and sign it, JEHOVAH GOD, would I put it aside and read it after the evening news was over? Of course not. I would open the letter reverently, read every comment, read every word deliberately, and when finished, I would probably read it over again. I would put it in a precious place, so that I would always have God's message before me.

You see the Bible is that letter, and we ought to be listening intensely because it is that truth that will shape us into His image. If God speaks to us through our circumstances or our mates, then we should pay close attention because God is communicating to us. Oftentimes, out of the same voice comes the same word, but in every spirit there is a different message. That is why we must listen aggressively.

Often after I give a particular series of messages, many people come up to me and thank the Lord for how He has been utilizing His Word and His truth to change their lives. They tell me, "I am beginning to see God from a whole different perspective." "I see that God accepts me the way I am." "I see that the cross is adequate." You see, they moved from passive listening to aggressive listening, and the result was that their entire lives were transformed.

Matthew 7:24 says, "Therefore whoever hears these sayings of Mine, and does them, I will liken him to a wise man who built his house on the rock." The solid foundation of our lives comes from aggressively hearing and implementing the Word of God. Nothing less will do. Anything less will cause our lives to be built upon shifting sand.

CONFORMED TO THE TRUTH

The second part of God's goal in communicating to us is that we may be conformed to the truth. In Romans 8:29 Paul wrote that the Lord has predestined us "to be conformed to the image of His Son."

How is God going to conform us to His image? By revealing the truth of His likeness. As we are confronted with the truth, we can do one of two things: we can refuse to be pushed into God's mold; or we can yield to Him and be fashioned into His likeness.

I once preached a series of sermons, "How the Truth Can Set You Free." God was working in my heart and I knew it. Week after week, people would come up to me and say, "I want to tell you how the Lord has set me free. I want to tell you how last week's message changed my life." Oftentimes when they would walk away, I would think to myself, *God, what about me? I'm the one who told them.* I knew I was not as free as God wanted me to be, even though I was sharing with other people how to be free. After months of being confronted by those whose lives were being changed, God changed my life in a remarkable way.

We are to listen in order to comprehend and to comprehend in order to be shaped and conformed to His truth. God never speaks in order to entertain us. God speaks that we may be made like Jesus. James wrote, "For if anyone is a hearer of the word and not a doer he is like a man observing his natural face in a mirror; for he observes himself, goes away, and immediately forgets what kind of man he was" (1:23-24). We are not simply to hear but also to obey—not simply to glance at the Word but also to grasp the Word. We are either in the process of resisting God's truth or in the process of being shaped and molded by His truth.

The apostle Paul's protégé, Timothy, is an excellent example of an individual's being conformed to the truth. After spending several years with Paul, he was assigned to shepherd the work of the gospel in Ephesus and Asia Minor. It was in this context that Paul wrote in his first letter, "Let no one despise your youth, but be an example to the believers in word, in conduct, in love, in spirit, in faith, in purity" (1 Tim. 4:12).

In his second epistle to Timothy, Paul penned these words, "When I call to remembrance the genuine faith that is in you, which dwelt first in your grandmother Lois and your mother Eunice, and I am persuaded is in you also" (2 Tim. 1:5).

Timothy didn't just *know* the truth; he was transformed by its power in such a way that his life was a constant example of godliness. How? By the unfolding ministry of God's Word.

Paul explained in 2 Timothy 3:14-15, "But as for you, continue in the things which you have learned and been assured of, knowing from whom you have learned them, and that from childhood you have known the Holy Scriptures, which are able to make you wise for salvation through faith which is in Christ Jesus."

COMMUNICATE THE TRUTH

The third objective God has in speaking is that we may communicate His truth. God never gives us anything to keep for ourselves. Whether it is money, insight, or truth, it has to be shared. Jesus said in His great command in Matthew 28:19–20, "Go therefore and make disciples of all the nations, baptizing them in the name of the Father and of the Son and of the Holy Spirit, teaching them to observe all things that I have commanded you." To those who witnessed His Ascension He declared in Acts 1:8, "But you shall receive power when the Holy Spirit has come upon you; and you shall be witnesses to Me in Jerusalem, and in all Judea and Samaria, and to the end of the earth." Jesus very clearly let His disciples know that the truth He had taught them during the past three years was not to be kept in a personal reservoir of knowledge. They were to give away everything they had received.

Chuck Colson comes as close to exemplifying this as anyone I know of. A trusted member of Richard Nixon's White House staff, he became ensnared in the political embroilment now universally known as "Watergate." Calling upon the Lord out of his distress, he was born again into God's kingdom. He was sent to a federal corrections institution in Montgomery, Alabama, where the seed was planted for a vision which has since blossomed into a nationwide prison ministry, reaching thousands of men and women with the restoring gospel of Christ. Only as Colson consciously surrendered all and gave himself to selfless service did his ministry bear fruit. He became a servant, communicating the truth that had set him free.

In 2 Timothy 2:2 Paul admonished his young pupil

Timothy, "And the things that you have heard from me among many witnesses, commit these to faithful men who will be able to teach others also." Timothy was to communicate the truth he had learned through Paul's instructions to others who would, in turn, pass it along.

In 2 Corinthians 5:20 Paul noted that we are "ambassadors for Christ." The sole purpose of ambassadors is to relay policies and decisions of their superiors to the people of the countries they are assigned to. So it is that we have an obligation to declare to others the divine plan and scriptural policies of our Master.

Each of us communicates something every waking moment by what we say and what we don't say, by what we do and what we fail to do. A son asks his father, "Well, Dad, how much are we going to tithe this Sunday?" Dad says, "We are not going to tithe this Sunday because I can't afford it. I've got too many bills to pay, and I simply can't use any of our money to tithe."

The father is communicating a lie to his son. Although not directly, he is communicating that we cannot trust God with our money, that God is not faithful to meet our needs, that God will not keep His promise concerning the tithe. A father who never reads the Bible is communicating that he is smart enough to make his own decisions without input from God's counsel. He teaches his family that a person can get along quite fine, thank you, without the advice and wisdom of God. The child who never sees the parents praying learns that fellowship with God is not required, that it is not necessary to ask Him about the important matters of life, that trials and tribulations can be handled without any direction from God.

On the other hand, a father talks to his family and says, "Well, God wants us to raise the amount we give. We are going to trust the Lord to provide us with the funds that we must have, and expect Him to meet our needs." That father is saying that we can depend upon God in every facet of life—when we can't see our way clear, God will work things out for us and be sufficient for our problems.

Often, even when we remain silent, we subtly state something. This was the case of the apostle Peter. Though recognizing the Gentiles as rightful recipients of God's grace, he developed the bad habit of withdrawing from meals whenever the Gentiles sat down to eat. Pressure from the Jews had its effect on him.

Though he was never outspoken in the matter, his prideful practice was soon picked up on by other Jews with the result "that even Barnabas was carried away with their hypocrisy" (Gal. 2:13). Without a word, Peter had effectively sent a message to those around him that the Gentiles were inferior. His actions said it all.

We must be honest in evaluating our responses to God's communications. Considering what God has graciously taught us over the years, are we deliberately applying these truths to our lives on a daily basis? When we comprehend the truth, are we conforming ourselves to the image of Christ? Are we then communicating this truth to others?

CHAPTER THREE

How God Gets Our Attention

PEOPLE REMEMBER WORLD War II for many reasons, but as a small child in Virginia, I particularly recall the shrill civil defense sirens that could pierce the air at any time of day. No matter what activity I was engaged in, the blast of the siren riveted my attention.

Similarly, when God speaks to us, we must recognize that His message is of utmost importance, deserving our full and complete concentration. Lest we become dull and insensitive to His Voice, God has His ways of gaining our undivided attention!

When we walk in the Spirit, our spiritual antennas are alert to God, and we can hear what He is saying. This is the normal Christian life, living keenly responsive to the Voice of God in whatever fashion He may choose to speak to us. We can be involved with our businesses or our families and hear God say something, and we immediately know what to do.

The problem is that we don't always walk in the Spirit. There are times when we choose to do things our own way. We are headed so fast in a given direction that if God spoke, we couldn't hear Him because we simply are not tuned in to Him.

God is aware of this problem. To rectify it, He uses many ways of getting our total, absolute attention to what He wants to communicate. More than likely you will discover that God has already used one or more of these principles in your life to get your attention. Perhaps you will discover the solution to a problem that has been hampering your spiritual effectiveness over a period of time. You may find that the problem you thought you had was simply God's way of trying to get you to focus on Him.

A RESTLESS SPIRIT

The sixth chapter of Esther is a beautiful example of God's working through a restless spirit. In this case, it involved King Ahasuerus who had been unwittingly duped by his prime minister, Haman. Because Haman hated all Jews, especially Esther's relative, Mordecai, he had tricked the king into signing an edict for the destruction of the Jews—men, women, and children—all in one day.

After he had signed the proclamation, the king could not sleep because of a restless spirit. Esther 6:1 reports, "That night the king could not sleep. So one was commanded to bring the book of the records of the chronicles; and they were read before the king."

Then the king discovered that Mordecai, whom Haman wanted to kill (along with the other Jews), had actually saved the king's life earlier by reporting a death plot by two men. Instead of the Jews being killed, Haman was executed and Mordecai honored. And it all started with a restless spirit, sent by the Lord to King Ahasuerus.

I believe *one of the simplest ways God can get our attention is to make us restless.* We may be going about our vocations, or our church or home lives when a restlessness begins to stir within our spirits. We can't put a finger on it; we don't know why it is there; we can't identify it, we don't even know exactly what is happening—but we have an uneasiness in our hearts. When such a time comes, the wise thing to do is to stop and ask the Lord what He is trying to say.

In my life, God frequently uses a persistent restlessness to direct me. I can look back and recall from my diary that every single time God has moved me from one pastorate to another, I have become restless for several months beforehand. It was His way of prompting me to seek Him so that when the time came, I would be ready to hear from Him. When you become restless in *your* spirit, don't run. Simply stop and listen to the Voice of God.

A WORD FROM OTHERS

A second way God gets our attention is speaking to us through others. Probably the best known example is Nathan's confrontation with David in 2 Samuel 12.

Having sinned against God in the incident with Bathsheba and Uriah, David apparently continued his reign without any visible evidence of a guilty conscience.

2 Samuel 12:1 sets the stage: "Then the LORD sent Nathan to David. And he came to him, and said...." God had given insight to Nathan which David desperately needed to hear.

I can remember one day when I was in the process of

making a decision, a friend stopped by the house. In our conversation, he informed me that God had spoken to him that morning in prayer and had given him a particular message for me. I was to spend the next day fasting and praying before I made my decision. Well, to begin with, he did not even know I was in the process of making a decision, so I quickly discerned God's hand in the matter. The next day I fasted and prayed. Before the day was over, God had given me very distinct direction that was absolutely contrary to my original thoughts.

That is why we must learn to listen with an open heart to the Voice of God as He speaks through others. If we are proud and egotistical and can't take direction from anyone, we need to read the book of Proverbs in which God repeatedly says that a man who cannot take criticism or reproof is destined for failure. Proverbs commends the man who learns to receive godly rebuke and thus succeeds in life.

However, we must be extremely careful in this regard, for sometimes others, no matter how well intentioned, can lead us astray. When Solomon's son, Rehoboam, became king, he sought counsel from the elders who had served his father. He needed advice in regard to a request from the people that he lighten the burden of service imposed by Solomon.

The elders advised Rehoboam to agree to the people's request and reap the rewards of kingly benevolence. Rather than listen, he went for further counsel from his own associates. They recommended he bring the people into even greater subjection.

He listened to the latter suggestion, and as a result, the nation of Israel split into the northern and southern kingdoms. It was a tragic decision. Heeding the voice of men who were not in right relationship with God cost him greatly. (See 2 Chron. 10.)

Therefore, while we surely know God speaks through other people, we must carefully examine both message and messenger. But, God has the power to know what is going on within us, and He has the power to place a burden upon someone else to say a word to us, even when the message doesn't appear logical at all.

BLESSINGS

A third way God speaks is through blessing us in most unusual ways. This is the sort of attention-getting method that I enjoy. Paul illustrated this in Romans 2:4 when he wrote: "Or do you despise the riches of His goodness, forbearance, and longsuffering, not knowing that the goodness of God leads you to repentance?."

God can use unusual, abundant blessings to gain our attention. The blessings may be spiritual or financial, or they may have something to do with the home or a vocation. Whatever they are, God just seems to pile them upon us. God can't use that method on everyone, because selfish people would get more independent, more self-centered, and more self-seeking and would totally ignore God. But He does get our attention by blessing us because the motive behind each of His methods is His love for us.

He sees our future, He sees our present. He sees His plan for us. He sees our plan. He sees them on a collision course, and when that happens, out of an expression of His love, He will get our attention so that we might listen to Him and be saved from ultimate ruin.

Isn't that exactly what we do with our children? If we

saw our children headed for trouble, wouldn't we out of love do something to stop them? Wouldn't we give them a word of wisdom to protect them from wrecking their lives?

For instance, if you knew your son was beginning to hang around with a group of boys who were noted for their minor run-ins with the law, wouldn't you sit down with him and warn him of the dangers involved? Wouldn't you urge him to make sure his friends had a positive influence on his life, and wouldn't you convey the fact that "bad company corrupts good morals"? Of course, you would. You would go to great lengths to establish proper bearings for your son to steer his life by, and God does no less for us.

UNANSWERED PRAYER

The fourth method God uses to get our attention is through unanswered prayer. As long as our petitions are sufficiently granted, we can cruise along, enjoying God's blessings and provision. But when a particularly urgent need arises and the heavens are brass, God has our complete attention.

Often, such seeming silence is a ripe time to conduct a spiritual self-examination under the illumination of the Holy Spirit. God's Word indicates there are reasons why some supplications are not answered—asking for the wrong reasons (James 4:3), disobedience (1 John 3:22), asking out of the will of God (1 John 5:14), among others. We should ask God if any of these problems have affected us.

According to 1 Peter 3:7, unanswered or unfruitful prayer can even stem from insensitivity in a marriage relationship. Peter stated that a husband's prayers are "'hindered" if he isn't loving his wife as he should.

At times God refuses to answer our prayers because He knows that if He answers them, we will stray further off base. That is why Satan will be more than happy to help us get an answer to everything we want outside the will of God, because he knows pleasure today may mean trouble tomorrow. Closed doors to prayer may sometimes be a sign of God's hand working to redirect our focus to another needful area of our lives.

The Lord used Paul's thorn as a teaching tool that has ministered to countless millions of believers (see 2 Cor. 12:7). His prayer went unanswered, but at the same time, his focus shifted from considering the severity of his problem to a new understanding of God's grace. When Paul opened his letters with his familiar "grace and peace" salutation, he well knew the meaning of the phrase. Unanswered prayer brought Paul into a new dimension of dependence on God.

Disappointment

Numbers 14 depicts how God uses disappointment to cause us to heed His voice. In the preceding chapter, the nation of Israel, fresh out of Egyptian bondage, was headed to the Promised Land. Twelve spies were sent into the Promised Land, but they came back and gave a negative report. The committee voted ten to two against possessing what God had already promised to provide for them in battle.

Numbers 26–35 relates God's judgment upon the nation of Israel because of their unbelief and unwillingness to possess what God had provided for them. The people realized their mistake and attempted to rectify the problem with a change of heart. Numbers 14:40 says, "And they rose early in the morning and went up to the top of the mountain, saying, 'Here we are, and we will go up to the place which the LORD has promised, for we have sinned!' " Moses responds in verse 42, "Do not go up, lest you be defeated by your enemies, for the LORD is not among you."

Talk about getting their attention! The Israelites had just come out of Egyptian bondage. They had on their backs the stripes of the taskmasters of Egypt. They could still smell the same old food they had been eating for hundreds of years. Now, they stood on the threshold of a land flowing with milk and honey, which God had promised them, but unbelief blinded them.

There was a tremendous sense of letdown, followed by mourning and weeping. It was too late—but God got their attention. He showed them that their unbelief would cause every single adult to die wandering in the wilderness like that of Egypt.

Sometimes the greatest disappointments in life are God's attention-getters. You may be planning to marry; everything is all set. You've talked to the florist and the preacher, and then the other party calls it all off. Your world collapses, and you think, *God, what in the world are You doing! Why have You allowed this to happen in my life! What are You doing to me, God!* It may well be that God in His loving plan reached down and stopped the wrong marriage and the disappointment got your attention. Otherwise, you might have continued doing what you thought was right, rather than doing the will of God.

We frequently have the tendency to blame God for our disappointments, making Him the object of our wrath.

When Job was engulfed with disaster, his wife mocked him, saying, "Do you still hold to your integrity? Curse God and die!" (Job 2:9). Satan obviously was at work trying to distort Job's view of God.

Job responded with this marvelous statement: "Shall we indeed accept good from God, and not accept adversity?" (v. 10). His attitude toward the extreme disappointment and heartache was amazing.

Thus, the way we respond to disappointment is extremely important. We allow Satan to point his ugly finger at us and tell us that we are not worth anything, that God doesn't really love us anymore. I have heard people say this for years. When great disappointment comes, they wring their hands and become angry and bitter toward God. They fail to realize that God saved them from ruining their lives. The wise response when disappointment comes is always to ask God what He is trying to teach us and then respond to our disappointments with new insight into God's plans and purposes.

UNUSUAL CIRCUMSTANCES

Unusual circumstances, the fifth method to get our attention, often cause us to turn our eyes and hearts to God. The story of Moses is a vivid example. Moses had grown up in Pharaoh's household. No doubt he was a tremendous warrior and a competent military strategist. One day, however, he decided to take things into his own hands—he killed an Egyptian soldier. He fled for his life, and the next forty years he spent on the backside of the desert in Midian, wearing the same old odorous clothes and tending a small bunch of sheep.

Because Moses was a strong-willed man and had to be

broken, God got his attention. We read in Exodus 3:1,2:

> Now Moses kept the flock of Jethro his father-in-law, the priest of Midian. And he led the flock to the back of the desert, and came to Horeb, the mountain of God. And the Angel of the LORD appeared to him in a flame of fire from the midst of a bush. So he looked, and behold, the bush burned with fire, but the bush was not consumed.

Moses had seen lots of fires and lots of burning bushes, but he had never seen a bush that blazed and was not consumed! His response was recorded in Exodus in verses 3 and 4:

> Then Moses said, "I will now turn aside and see this great sight, why the bush does not burn." So when the LORD saw that he turned aside to look, God called to him from the midst of the bush, and said, "Moses, Moses!" And he said, "Here I am."

Out of an unusual experience, God got his attention. Moses had to stop his daily routine to see what was going on. When he did, God spoke to him.

We must learn to live for the presence of God in every circumstance of life. A child of God, walking in the Spirit, is to look for the handiwork, the footprint, and the handprint of almighty God in every single situation of life. God is sovereign, and we are His children. There is no such thing as an accident in the life of a child of God. There are some things God may allow. There are some things that God sends. There are attention-getters that God brings into our lives, but there are no accidents.

Suppose your boss said that he was going to have to let you go. You can respond in one of several ways. You can wonder what other people are going to think about it or why God allowed this to happen. Or you can ask God what He is trying to teach you. Since God is in everything in some fashion, even in such a sticky situation, the proper response is for you as a believer to get God's perspective. The same God who gave you the job is the One who allowed it to be taken away.

God knows exactly what it takes to get our attention, and often it is through highly unusual circumstances that we stand back and take note of what God is doing in our lives.

Failure

God uses the circumstance of failure to get our attention. The nation of Israel had already come to the Promised Land. Their first responsibility was to take the city of Jericho, which they did. Their next challenge was Ai, a small, sleepy town just up the road from Jericho. From all natural points of view, Ai would be a pushover compared to Jericho. But the Israelite warriors made two terrible mistakes.

First, God told Joshua that all the booty and gold and silver in the city of Jericho was His. However, one man, Achan, decided to keep some of the treasure for himself, and he buried it underneath his tent.

Second, when the Israelites went to Ai, the Scripture implies they simply decided to conquer it; they had no real military strategy, no real direction from God. Overconfident, they sent a small band of soldiers to quickly dispose of Ai. Joshua 7:5 describes the unexpected result: "The men of Ai struck down thirty-six men, for they chased them from before the gate...and struck them down on the descent; therefore the hearts of the people melted and became like water." The mighty Israelites had been defeated. And, no doubt, much fear gripped them because news of their catastrophe would spread throughout the land. Joshua's response was recorded in verse 6: "Then Joshua tore his clothes, and fell to the earth on his face before the ark of the LORD until evening, both he and the elders of Israel; and they put dust on their heads." You see, God got Joshua's attention by letting him fail in a military endeavor.

When God has blessed us spiritually or financially, when God has done something super in our lives, that is the time to remember Ai. His blessing should bring about a response of thanksgiving and praise and our precise attention, because following great blessings is the time for failure. It is just then that we must be ultrasensitive to the Voice of God, because all too often we become proud and egotistical and ruin God's purpose in blessing us.

As a result, He lets failure come. How many businessmen experience failure and wonder how it all happened? Then they simply turn right around and go straight back into the problem without seeking God's guidance on the matter.

I remember talking to a woman who described her experience with a home Bible study. Eager to reach her neighborhood for Christ, she stuffed dozens of mailboxes with invitations. When the day arrived, she was ready with several dozen baked goods and a couple of pots of coffee. Only three women came.

Rather than give up, though, she committed herself to finding a better way. After a few more attempts, she discovered the women responded far better with a personal invitation. Today several dozen excited people attend her home Bible studies. Failure became the stepping-stone to success.

There is a vast difference between failing and being a failure. A failure in a given incident could prove to be the greatest stepping-stone to success in our lives if we are wise enough in the midst of failure to give our attention to God. If failure today can make us a success tomorrow, we should be willing to fail in the small things to succeed in the larger ones. We simply must be willing to acknowledge our mistakes, tell God we blew it, and thank Him at the same time for gaining our wholehearted attention. Failing does not make us failures, but failing and then responding properly can pave the way to future victories.

Financial Collapse

Sometimes to get our attention, God dries up our finances. The whole theme of the book of Judges is "every one did what was right in his own eyes" (Judg. 17:6). Time after time the Israelites fell into idolatry and intermarriage with members of heathen tribes. Judges 6:1–6 described the scene:

> And the children of Israel did evil in the sight of the LORD. So the LORD delivered them into the hand of Midian for seven years, and the hand of Midian prevailed against Israel. Because of the Midianites, the children of Israel made for themselves the dens, the caves, and the strongholds which are in the mountains. So it was, whenever Israel had sown, Midianites would come up; also Amalekites and the people of the East would come up against them. Then they would encamp against them and destroy the produce of the earth as far as Gaza, and leave no sustenance for Israel, neither sheep nor ox nor donkey. For they would come up with their livestock and their tents, coming in as numerous as locusts; both they and their camels were without number; and they would enter the land to destroy it. So Israel was greatly impoverished because of the Midianites, and the children of Israel cried out to the LORD.

When did they cry out to the Lord? When God took away every material good they had and drove them into the dens and caves, where they hid for their lives. God knew exactly what it would take to get their attention— the destruction of all their material possessions.

Has God ever dried up your finances? At one time in your life your finances may have been like an ocean. Then they became like a sea; dried up to a river, trickled into a stream—and then they were gone. For the average man, this is often the toughest way for God to get his attention. Yet the believer's response is often faulty. He thinks if he tithes, God will not shrivel up his finances. However, if anyone tithes and deliberately disobeys God, God certainly uses monetary woes to make that person seek His face.

He did not contradict His Word either when He said through Paul, "My God will supply all your needs according to His riches in glory in Christ Jesus" (Phil. 4:19 NASB). He knows our greatest need is to listen to Him. That's far more important to God than any material gain.

I know several people whose finances God devastated. They had nothing left, but God had their attention. Such intervention forced them to face critical issues in their spiritual walk.

During World War II, industrialist R. G. K.'s machines were as much a part of the Allied success as the armed forces themselves. His gargantuan machinery, moving earth and rubble, paved the way for runways on several Pacific islands.

K. was also a committed Christian, and he made God his full partner in his business endeavors, giving to God and His work in superabundant fashion. In the late 1920s, however, when business was still growing for K., he decided to put what he termed "God's share" of the profits back into the business, promising God He would receive a bigger portion the following year.

The next two years were some of the worst K. experienced. Profits shrank. Debts mounted. Work projects became nightmares. Then K. remembered his earlier pledge to the Lord, reinstated it and, within a year, recovered from his financial reversals. God had used the red ink to gain his attention.

The issue is not how much money God does or does not take away. That has nothing to do with it. The issue is the means God uses to get our attention. The Israelites' response to their predicament was to cry out to God. God listened, delivered them from the Midianites, and blessed them.

Tragedy

Tragedy is sometimes a circumstantial method by which God gains our attention. Numbers 21:4–7 describes some events that happened to the Israelites.

> Then they journeyed from Mount Hor by the Way of the Red Sea, to go around the land of Edom; and the soul of the people became very discouraged on the way. And the people spoke against God and against Moses: "Why have you brought us up out of Egypt to die in the wilderness? For there is no food and no water, and our soul loathes this worthless bread." So the LORD sent fiery serpents among the people, and they bit the people; and many of the people of Israel died. Therefore the people came to Moses, and said, "We have sinned, for we have spoken against the LORD and against you; pray to the LORD that He take away the serpents from us." So Moses prayed for the people.

We can't always view tragedy in a person's life as a sign of God's disapproval, but we should look at every tragic situation through a spiritual filter. Though that is a difficult assignment, people such as Joni Eareckson Tada are living evidence of God's sovereign design in calamity.

When she was a young teenager, full of God's vibrancy, Joni's life was radically altered one summer afternoon when she dove into a pool of shallow water. In the twinkling of an eye she was introduced to the numb world of quadriplegics.

Months of despair in a hospital did little to bring any hope for her now-shaky future. The eternal question "How can God allow this?" danced on her lips day and night. Then steadily her faith in the love of God for her began to surmount her anxious and sometimes bitter queries.

In subsequent years, she developed the remarkable capacity to paint with a brush gripped in her teeth. Her heart for God grew by leaps and bounds and a ministry to millions began, a ministry birthed and nourished by tragedy. Her books, movies, lectures, and special outreach to the handicapped have made her overcoming life a familiar story to most Christians worldwide.

How many thousands of devoted Christians have been called to the ministry through the life of Jim Elliot? When he was killed by the Auca Indians in his late twenties, it seemed on the surface an untimely death and loss. Yet his wife's recounting of his life, heart, and actions for God in *Through Gates of Splendor, The Shadow of the Almighty,* and *The Journals of Jim Elliot* has been the spiritual catapult to thrust untold numbers into the fields "white for harvest" (John 4:35).

Sickness and Affliction

Hezekiah was a godly king. The Lord had blessed him on many occasions and had delivered him by striking down 185,000 invading Assyrians (see 2 Chron. 32). Verses 22 and 23 tell the jubilation that resulted.

Thus the Lord saved Hezekiah and the inhabitants of Jerusalem from the hand of Sennacherib the king of Assyria, and from the hand of all others, and guided them on every side. And many brought gifts to the Lord at Jerusalem and presents to Hezekiah king of Judah, so that he was exalted in the sight of all nations thereafter.

Then, suddenly, in verses 24 and 25 the scene darkens. "In those days Hezekiah was sick and near death, and he prayed to the Lord; and He spoke to him and gave him a sign. But Hezekiah did not repay according to the favor shown him, for his heart was lifted up; therefore wrath was looming over him and over Judah and Jerusalem."

Hezekiah became gravely ill. Why do you think he was struck with such sickness? I don't think God just "happened" to put in the verses the matter of Hezekiah's pride. He obviously gained Hezekiah's attention concerning his pride through his illness.

One way God uses to get our attention is through sickness or affliction. For example, God secured the attention of Saul of Tarsus on the Damascus road by knocking him to the ground and blinding his eyes. For three days he couldn't see anything. Wouldn't that get your attention?

I do believe in healing. I believe the Scripture in James 5:14 that says, "Is anyone among you sick? Let him call for the elders of the church, and let them pray over him, anointing him with oil in the name of the Lord."

When I was in the hospital for several weeks, God dealt with me wonderfully. He used my illness to painfully get my attention so that I would hear His voice. If someone had prayed for God to heal me, I would have missed one of the greatest spiritual times in my entire life. I needed to hear from God. We have to be very careful in the area of healing, because God will often use an illness to cause us to examine our lives.

As I look back in my diary, I see that in every instance when God allowed me to be physically immobilized, I had usually done something foolish to put me in that position, like picking up a wheelbarrow and hurting my back. Each time God brought me to a decision that had to be made and forced me to face an issue I would have avoided otherwise.

God doesn't use the same methods on everyone. He knows exactly what it takes in your life to get your attention—a restless spirit, a word from others, blessings, unanswered prayer, or unusual circumstances. He may use one today, and then He will employ a different one three weeks from now, something else months away, or an entirely different strategy two years from today.

What is important is that God cares enough to employ various and sundry methods to cause us to stop and listen to what He is saying. He is not about to let us walk into an open manhole without giving us clearly discernible danger signals. He is out to give us specific guidance and help us move into His wonderful plans and purposes for our lives.

He will not let us wander aimlessly through the snarled interchanges of everyday life without pointing us to the appropriate signposts He has already erected. He does so by gently speaking to us.

Our problem is not that we doubt God's ability and desire to communicate, but we are all too easily stumped as to how to identify His Voice. Since we are His sheep and His sheep "know His voice" (John 10:4), there must be some perceptible clues as to the nature of His conversation. Those clues will be explored in the next chapter.

CHAPTER FOUR

Identifying the Voice of God

PEOPLE OFTEN ASK me, "When I listen to God how do I know if it is God speaking or some other voice?" Or, "I've asked the Lord to give me direction, but it's as if I hear two voices. How do I know if God is the One I hear or if Satan is involved? Or am I just talking to myself?" Or, "Is it just my conscience playing games with me? Or is God trying to get through?"

Those are legitimate questions that need to be answered. Identifying who is doing the talking is essential if we are to listen accurately.

In Matthew 16 Jesus told His disciples that He must go to Jerusalem, suffer many things, be killed, and then be raised up on the third day (v. 21). Peter, though with obvious good intentions, took affront at Jesus' remarks and said, "Far be it from You, Lord; this shall not happen to You!" (v. 22). Jesus turned to Peter and stated, "Get behind Me, Satan! You are an offense to Me, for you are not mindful of the things of God, but the things of men" (v. 23).

In this passage you can see the difference between the Voice of God and the voice of Satan. Peter's dilemma in this instance is also ours. We may seek the Lord's mind about decisions we have to make concerning our families, our finances, our vocations. We may be committed to doing the right thing, so we begin to pray. Today we feel we should move in one direction, but tomorrow we feel we should move in the opposite direction. It seems as if the voice we hear tells us something different each day. The result is our frustration and confusion. We wonder how we can know positively whose voice we hear.

Jesus made it clear in John 10:27 that the believer's normal experience is to hear God accurately. "My sheep hear My voice, and I know them, and they follow Me." If we as believers walk in the Spirit, understand the meaning of the Cross, and allow the Holy Spirit to fill us and live His life through us, then it should be easy for us to distinguish whether the voice we hear is of God, the flesh, or the devil. The natural walk of Spirit-filled, committed believers is such that when God speaks, we can identify His Voice.

Some mature Christians have had experience in listening to God, and they can distinguish between God's Voice and another's. For others, especially young Christians, it is a bit more of a problem. A sheep who has been with a shepherd for many years is better equipped to hear the shepherd's voice, but that is not true for the newborn lamb. Since we know that the holy Scriptures teach us that all believers, young and old, should clearly discern the Voice of God, let's look at some scriptural guidelines that will help us determine the mind of God as we sift through what seem to be conflicting voices.

CONSISTENT WITH THE WORD

God's Voice will never tell us to engage in any activity or relationship that is inconsistent with the holy Scriptures. For example, I hear people say, "When I pray I feel so guilty. I feel condemned. I imagine God is pointing His finger at me, and I have great difficulty in asking Him for anything."

If our sins are confessed, our lives are clean (as far as we know), we are not involved in any disobedience, and we *still* feel guilty and condemned, then that voice is strictly from the devil. We know that to be true because Romans 8:1 informs us, "There is therefore now no condemnation to those who are in Christ Jesus." The accusing voice is totally inconsistent with the written Word of God; thus the guilt is false and is a dart of satanic condemnation.

That is why if we neglect the Word of God and don't build it into our lives, when Satan comes along we're all too easily deceived. Since almighty God never tells us to do anything to contradict His Word, the better we know it, the more readily we will identify His speaking Voice.

If you're in the process of making a decision about a relationship, go to the Word of God and see what He says about relationships. If it's about finances, see what the Word of God says about finances. Whatever your need, some portion of Scripture can offer you godly guidance. If what you hear in prayer is not consistent with Scripture, then what you hear is not God; it's another voice—that of Satan and his host or that of the flesh. The Voice of God will never include any data that violate the principles of Scripture.

CONFLICT WITH HUMAN WISDOM

Although there are exceptions, usually when God requires something of you, it will clash with what you consider to be the natural, reasonable course of action. Jesus said that if a fellow strikes you on one cheek, you should turn the other (see Matt. 5:39). Now that's not reasonable. He also said that if someone wants you to go one mile, you should cheerfully go two miles. That's not reasonable either.

The prophet Isaiah put it this way:

> "For my thoughts are not your thoughts, Nor are your ways My ways," says the LORD. "For as the heavens are higher than the earth, So are My ways higher than your ways, And My thoughts than your thoughts" (Isa. 55:8).

Jesus usually did the opposite of what people expected. If we feel the tug of the world and what we hear from God seems reasonable and rational, then we should check it out. That's not to say that God doesn't utilize human wisdom. He does. But on many occasions God's Voice will ask us to accomplish something that seems quite illogical to our rational minds.

This was so when God told Abraham to sacrifice his son. Abraham could have reasoned that this command was of the devil, that God would never tell him to do such a thing. But it *was* of God, and because he obeyed, God continued to multiply Abraham's seed through his son Isaac.

CLASH WITH FLESHLY NATURE

God will never tell us to do anything that gratifies the flesh. I don't mean to say that God isn't for fun. He is, but He is for fun in the right way that pleases Him and brings wholesome fulfillment, not instantaneous gratification of the flesh.

If what we hear urges us to gratify the flesh, to forget what anyone else says, just do as we please, then we should know that it isn't of God. He doesn't speak in those terms. God always speaks in such a way that the results please the Spirit of God within us, not the flesh. The old sensual nature is a part of our physical lives, but it is to be under the control of the Holy Spirit. We are to satisfy the yearning of the Spirit; His Voice will build up and edify our spirits, not our fleshly natures.

Our present society continually appeals to that fleshly nature. Television, magazines, and many businesses seek to affect the individual by arousing carnal instincts. It is in a world dominated by such carnal clattering that God calls us to listen to a Voice that always seeks the benefit of others as well as ourselves, a Voice that requires substantial faith to hear.

CHALLENGE TO FAITH

God is always challenging our faith, and in so doing He builds our relationship with Him and helps us grow into intimacy with Him. When we lift up our petitions to the Lord, we should always ask ourselves if they will challenge our faith. Not every decision we make will necessarily call for great faith, but in making those decisions in which we aren't sure if we are hearing from God, asking this question will help us determine the origin of the voice.

When Jesus was on earth, He was always looking for people to respond in faith. He could just speak and that would be the end of it, but in many instances His Voice requires an act of faith on our part to comprehend what He has revealed.

COURAGE

When God speaks, oftentimes His Voice will call for an act of courage on our part. Probably nowhere is this courage more exemplified than in the book of Joshua. Joshua was faced with the staggering mission of getting hordes of grumbling Israelites across the Jordan River when the Lord delivered him an encouraging message (Josh. 1:1–9).

In the space of those nine verses, God exhorted Joshua to spiritual courage no less than three times:

"Be strong and of good courage, for to this people you shall divide as an inheritance the land" (Josh. 1:6).

"Only be strong and very courageous" (Josh. 1:7).

"Have I not commanded you? Be strong and of good courage" (Josh. 1:9).

I would say Joshua needed courage to obey God's command, wouldn't you? Just think if you were following in the footsteps of a man named Moses. Despite Moses' miraculous leadership, even he had failed to take the Israelites into the Promised Land! Joshua needed some spiritual fortitude to complete the task. No less today do we stand in need of inner valor if we are to accomplish the works God has assigned us.

The disciples needed courage to respond to Jesus' command, "Follow Me." Paul needed courage to preach to those who had once hated him. Gideon needed courage to defeat his adversaries. When God speaks, the fulfillment of His plans hinges to some degree on whether we respond with confident, courageous spirits. His Voice leads us not into timid discipleship but into bold witness.

REVIEW

Let's now apply these five points to Matthew 16 and see how they are related. First, was Jesus' statement that He was going to die consistent with Scripture? Yes, according to Isaiah 53, it was. Second, did Jesus' statement conflict with human wisdom? Was His assertion that He would be killed and rise again on the third day at odds with human logic? Obviously so.

Third, did Jesus' remark clash with Peter's fleshly desires? It certainly did, because Peter saw himself as one of the group of disciples, and if Jesus died, where would that leave Peter? He would no doubt be left out. Fourth, did Jesus' reply challenge Peter's faith and require his courage? It certainly did. Peter had seen a lot in his life, Jesus' resurrection proclamation was a monumental challenge to his faith. Would he be willing to follow a man who said He was the Messiah but would soon lose His life? Would he have the courage to persevere and, if He rose, to follow Him? God's voice obviously called for courage.

Even though Jesus was obviously the speaker in this passage, Peter responded by declaring that what He said would never happen. Jesus told Peter he wasn't setting his mind on God's interest but on man's, and He told Satan to get behind Him. Jesus knew that Satan had objected to His death on the cross through Peter's lips.

I'm sure that Peter, in his enthusiasm and excitement, said what he did as an expression of loyalty and faithfulness. The only problem was, *it wasn't from God.*

What we must clearly recognize is that Satan is a master of deceit. Through his craftiness and deceitfulness, he lured Eve and Adam into rebellion against God in the Garden of Eden. Satan was deceptive in the way he spoke then and still is today. As maturing believers, if we listen to God, He will not lead us into the wrong decisions. He will protect us as we learn to walk in the Spirit and understand the centrality of the Cross.

We can distinguish the Voice of God from the voice of Satan, despite Satan's ability to cloak his voice expertly. He comes as an angel of light along with all the appropriate enticements. That's exactly why believers also can be deceived. Multitudes of God's people today live in satanic deception, thinking they've heard from God. There are church-going people who say they have heard from God, and God has revealed that Jesus Christ *isn't* the Son of God. That isn't true, of course. The Bible says, "Beloved, do not believe every spirit, but test the spirits, whether they are of God....Every spirit that confesses that Jesus Christ has come in the flesh is of God, and every spirit that does not confess that Jesus Christ has come in the flesh is not of God" (1 John 4:1–3).

As the age grows darker, more voices will be detrimental to the people of God. Those who reluctantly seek Him and don't intentionally desire to know Him will be easily swayed to accept numerous doctrinal errors.

Satan doesn't knock on the front door and say, "Hi, I'm Satan." He comes in the backdoor using the most cunning, convincing, persuasive language possible. *The best way in the world to deceive believers is to cloak a message in religious language* and declare that it conveys some new insight from God.

That's why as believers we should continue to mature so that we don't need anyone else to teach us. Although God has sent pastors as teachers, the personal feeding of our spiritual beings should be our number-one priority. We don't always have to have someone else to tell us what God is saying about a decision. We all, of course, need counsel occasionally, but on a regular basis we should be able to become humble before God and know the difference between God's Voice and the devil's voice, between God's ways and the world's ways.

There are several other ways by which we can distinguish the divine nature of God's Voice.

THE EFFECTS ON OTHER PEOPLE

God is concerned about the influence and witness we as believers have on other people. If there is a harshness or crudeness toward others in what we hear, then it's not from God. God never talks about our lives. He talks about our surrender. He talks about our yieldedness. He talks about our crucifixion, our death. He talks about loving our brother, about bearing one another's burdens, about encouraging one another, about not causing others to stumble. Satan tells us that we can do what we want, that we shouldn't worry about the rippling effects of our lives on other people. He tells us every man is an island unto himself, and we should please number one only.

When God speaks, He will have not only our best interests in mind but also the good of all concerned. He always works for the good of all His people, not just a few.

PATIENCE

Nowhere in Scripture does God tell anyone to rush into a decision. He doesn't operate that way. Anyone in the financial world knows that success is not based on snap decisions. Though there may be times when we need to hear from God quickly, God will never tell us to rush in blindly. We may have to move swiftly, but we can move swiftly in the will of God and still not hurry into a situation.

Satan always encourages us to act immediately, because he knows if we back off and think long enough, we'll reconsider. How many people have made decisions they regretted for the rest of their lives? Psalm 27:14 exhorts us, "Wait on the LORD; Be of good courage, And He shall strengthen your heart; Wait, I say, on the LORD!" Psalm 62:5 explains, "My soul, wait silently for God alone, For my expectation is from Him."

If we feel an overwhelming urge to act spontaneously, we better pull in the reins. God is interested in having all the details in their proper places.

King Saul was one who lost his throne because he acted hastily. Chosen by the Lord to be king over Israel, he was instructed by the prophet Samuel to wait at Gilgal. "Seven days you shall wait, till I come to you and show you what you should do" (1 Sam. 10:8).

On the seventh day, Samuel still hadn't arrived. With a hostile Philistine army pressing in on him, Saul decided to take matters in his own hands, and he prepared burnt offerings to invoke the Lord's favor. As soon as the offering was completed, Samuel appeared. Saul offered some lame excuses, but his rashness disqualified him for a long and peaceful reign. Getting ahead of God is a terrible mistake, and the consequences are always distasteful.

On the other hand, Nehemiah, cupbearer to Persian King Artaxerxes, patiently waited for God's timing with glorious results. Having heard from exiles who had been living in occupied Judah that the walls of Jerusalem were in shambles, a grieved Nehemiah "sat down and wept, and mourned for many days; I was fasting and praying before the God of heaven" (Neh. 1:4).

Rather than dash into instant action, Nehemiah waited before God. In fact, he beseeched the Lord for a period of four months, until one day the king himself asked Nehemiah why his appearance was downcast. Nehemiah explained the situation, and within days, he was off to Jerusalem with the king's approval and all the necessary building materials. Nehemiah waited until God put all the particulars in place and then moved.

CONSIDER THE CONSEQUENCES

Satan tells us to "move on, go ahead, make the decision, don't worry about the consequences." God, however, is interested and concerned about the ramifications of our actions. As we look back on our lives, how many of us, if we had considered the consequences of a decision, would have made the same choice? Surely we would all like to take a few back.

Had Abraham weighed the possible ramifications of his dealings with Hagar, no doubt he would have resisted Sarah's pleas to produce a child with her maid.

Had David thought of the severity of God's discipline with him over the numbering of his subjects in Israel and Judah, he would have listened to the far-less-discerning Joab's advice to cease and desist the entire project.

Satan urges us to "eat, drink, and be merry." But he fails to add "for tomorrow you are going to die and face judgment." Satan is not the kind of fellow who would remind us of Scripture.

The New Testament is clear in considering the consequences of decisions. Whenever God speaks, He has our future in mind and He will cause each of us to ask, "If I make this decision, what will happen to my family, to my job, to my walk with the Lord?" God isn't just the God of today, He's also the God of tomorrow.

GODLY COUNSEL

God often leads us to get advice from others. When He does, He wants us to check out the life-style of that person from whom we receive counsel. Why should a believer go to a nonbeliever to get advice that will affect his life? Some businessmen may have a problem with that, but I challenge you to consider the spiritual, moral, and behavioral track record of anyone from whom you obtain advice. That decision you make affects not just your job but also your entire family and future.

That is not to say unsaved people have no wisdom or good advice. However, the believer can add the dimension of spiritual and scriptural insight into the matter at hand. Some counselors dispense unscriptural advice that will lead to ruin and destruction.

Proverbs has a lot to say about the value of wise counsel. Proverbs 13:10 declares, "By pride comes only contention, But with the well-advised is wisdom." Proverbs 20:5 instructs, "Counsel in the heart of man is like deep water, But a man of understanding will draw it out."

I remember when my grandfather, who was a minister, told me one day, "Charles, whatever you do in life, always obey God fully. If He tells you to run your head through a brick wall, go forward, expecting Him to make a hole." I have never forgotten that advice, and it has been a main girder of truth that has supported my personal ministry over the last three decades.

SPIRITUAL GROWTH

God informs us that He has ordained, foreordained, and predestined us to become conformed to the image of Christ. That being so, then whatever God speaks to us will stimulate our spiritual growth. That means that God will never tell us to do anything or think of anything that sets us back spiritually.

He would never tell us to pursue a course of action that would hinder our spiritual maturity. One young woman came to me and told me she was dating a man who was an alcoholic and an adulterer. Despite this, she informed me that she believed God had told her to marry him. Was she hearing God's Voice? Of course not, because a marriage of that nature simply would not contribute to her spiritual growth. In fact, more often than not, such a situation is to the detriment of the believer.

PEACE

When God speaks, one of the most prevalent signs is a sense of calmness in the spirit. It may not be tranquil at first. In fact, it may be full of conflict and strife, but the longer we listen, the quieter and more peaceful our spirits become. We begin to possess what the apostle Paul called a peace "which surpasses all understanding" (Phil. 4:7). It is a peace that surrounds us like a fortress and keeps us from being overwhelmed with anxiety, worry, and frustration.

The process of being elected president of the Southern Baptist Convention was one of the most tumultuous conflicts in my life; yet I had perfect peace. Months beforehand, I had prayed and sought the mind of the Lord as to what I should do regarding the possibility of being nominated as president. On occasion, I spent a week at a time praying, being quiet and listening to God. On the night before the Convention met, I again waited upon the Lord and listened to Him. As a result of His guidance, I allowed my name to be nominated. There was great turmoil, and great conflict ensued immediately thereafter. In the midst of all that, I had perfect peace and assurance. The time that I had wrestled with the Lord and listened to Him assured me that I must allow my name to be placed in nomination. Those weeks and months of praying and searching were the sure foundation that caused me to know I had done the right thing when the moment of crisis came.

When that sort of peace comes to us, we know we've heard from God, and we are confident it is His Voice. When an individual comes to me and indicates he has heard from God on a particular subject, yet he seems disturbed about the whole situation, I question whether he has truly heard from Him. People who have truly heard from God usually don't try to convince me that God has spoken to them; they simply know that the decision was of God.

We will never have God's peace about disobedience. We may be able to believe with our minds, but we will never be able to believe with our spirits and exercise faith.

Colossians 3:15 says:

> And let the peace (soul harmony which comes) from the Christ rule (act as umpire continually) in your hearts—deciding and settling with finality all questions that arise in your minds—[in that peaceful state] to which [as members of Christ's] one body you were also called [to live]. And be thankful—appreciative, giving praise to God always (AMPLIFIED).

When I was a child growing up, my mother would tell me, "Charles, dinner will be ready at 6:00 P.M. Be here." Pretty soon I would get involved in playing and 6:00 came. All of a sudden I would hear a voice crying, "Charles, Charles!" I didn't have to wonder if that was my mother's voice. I knew in a split second whose it was. I had grown up hearing it. A thousand mothers could have called my name, but only *my* mother would have called my name in such a way that got my attention. When we are saved, it is a natural, normal behavior to know that when God speaks; it is our Father who has called us by name.

───────────────

CHAPTER FIVE

Factors That Determine How God Communicates

SINCE WE HAVE determined that God still speaks through various means, what determines the content of what God says? Let's take two groups of people praying about the same thing. Group *A* might hear a very positive response from God, while Group *B* might be almost negative and defeated. Why is Group *A* motivated and encouraged, while Group *B* is discouraged? God loves both groups equally, but there is a radical difference in what they hear. That difference can usually be explained through three primary factors that significantly influence the substance of what God communicates to His children.

OUR RELATIONSHIP WITH HIM

The first factor, our relationship with God, affects what we hear when we pray and listen. The only message an unbeliever will ever hear from God is that he is a sinner who needs to look to Jesus as his Savior. Until that person knows Christ as his personal Messiah, he will not hear God speak on any subject other than salvation.

What about believers? How does our relationship with Him influence what we hear. That relationship is twofold. *First of all, we are saved.* When we by faith receive Him as our personal Savior, the Bible says we are born again. We are taken from the kingdom of darkness and placed into the kingdom of light. We become the children of God. Our salvation experience is the beginning of our relationship with God.

The second part of that relationship is our identification. Our salvation takes care of our eternal security, and our identification takes care of our daily walk of victory. By identification, I mean that Christ's life is now mine and mine His. "It is no longer I who live, but Christ lives in me" (Gal. 2:20). What happened to Christ at Calvary happened to me. Christ was crucified, I was crucified. Christ was buried, I was buried. Christ was raised, I was raised. Identification is the theme song of Romans 6. When we are identified with Him and have accepted that by faith sin's power is broken, we are free to walk in the Spirit, liberated to become the persons God wants us to be. It is Christ Jesus living His life in us and through us as individuals. Our relationship to Him is that we are saved, we are forgiven, we are accepted, we are children of God. We are secure in the Cross. We can have the peace and assurance that our daily walk is pleasing and honorable to Him. These two relationships, salvation and identification, make a difference in what we hear from God.

One who is safe and secure in the love of God and sustained by His grace no longer hears from a distant God.

He now listens to Someone who loves him enough to bring him to a personal relationship, and that makes all the difference. We no longer come to Him, groping and pleading, wondering if we are accepted by Him or not.

Through my identification with Him, I come, knowing that I am accepted not by my behavior but by my belief in Him because of what He has already accomplished. Thus I can approach Him with boldness and assurance.

He is now my personal, faithful, and merciful High Priest. He is my Father with whom I enjoy intimate communion. I no longer have to stand on the perimeter, peering into His presence. Jesus has paid the price of admission through His shed blood so that I now am a legal member of His own family, sitting daily before Him secure in my sonship. I hear His voice because I am the "sheep of His pasture" (see Ps. 79:13).

OUR UNDERSTANDING OF HIM

What we hear is affected not only by our relationship with Him but also by another factor—our understanding of who He is. We were born with a mental grid system into which were placed positive or negative choices. We unconsciously accepted viewpoints based primarily on what others taught us. Our viewpoint of God was greatly colored by that of our parents and what we were taught early in life. Many of us incorporated into our inner selves concepts of God handed down to us by school-teachers, Sunday-school personnel, and preachers. Our perception of God today is still comprised to a large degree of their understanding.

One morning after a speaking engagement, two young men were taking me to the airport. The driver began talking to me. He told me he had received a tape of a sermon that I had preached on putting away childish things. He informed me that he had driven for over sixteen hours, and throughout the whole trip he had listened to the tape. He was amazed at the difference that had come over his life after hearing it and how his relationship with his parents and with the Lord had been strengthened through the message.

The other young man was quiet for most of the trip, but as we neared the airport, he opened up. He indicated that he wasn't sure what God was doing in his life, and some of the confusion he had concerned his call to the ministry. When he finished speaking, I asked him about his relationship with his parents. He responded that his father was a very domineering man. Then, without any provocation, he burst out, "You know, when I come before God to pray, I get the same withering feeling as when I talk to my father. It's as if I see my father when I talk to God. I have the same image of a dominant God who has not accepted me, and before Him I feel I can never measure up."

Multitudes of people approach God in the same fearful way, because their notion of God has been distorted by the attitude, behavior, or instruction of others. It's easy to see how our understanding of who God is affects what we hear. In fact, I have identified seven key areas in understanding the nature of God. These determine the essence of the communication we receive from Him.

Loving or Demanding Father

When God speaks, do we hear a loving Father who forgives us and has a genuine interest in us? Or do we hear a demanding parent who is always raising the standard on us, expecting us to measure up to great expectations? Do we hear the Voice of One who accepts us where we are, or do we hear someone who is constantly beseeching us to makes A's instead of B's. When we pray, do we come before a Father who wraps His arms around us in a loving embrace or do we stand feeling condemned?

Each of us listens to one of these: We hear a loving, accepting Father who says, "That is okay. Just trust Me next time, and I will make your joy full"; or we hear a demanding father who upbraids us, saying, "Well, you've messed it up again, haven't you? You certainly didn't do what I told you, did you?"

The latter portrayal is not the God of the Bible. The former is. In fact, our security as believers is often wrapped up in understanding that the God we serve is first and foremost the *God of love.*

Intimate or Distant Friend

When we hear God, do we listen to an intimate Friend or to a distant friend only casually acquainted with us? Intimacy is a vital part of the Christian life. God wants to build intimacy with us. One of the evident proofs is that He came in the Person of Jesus Christ to walk as a Man among men.

Today when we think of intimacy, most people think only of sex. But the greatest intimacy is that of friendship, emotional intimacy. When we pray and talk to God, we listen to an intimate Friend, One who shares with us what we want to share and One who listens to us. He is a true, genuine, and faithful Friend.

He is always there, we can always count on Him. A distant friend may give ear to our prayers if we happen to be interested in the same things he's concerned about, but an intimate Friend is One who listens, whether or not the subject matter is of great interest. Understanding God as an intimate Friend or as a distant acquaintance influences the degree of openness we have in our conversations with Him.

As a newspaper delivery boy, I had a teacher who would stop on the side of the street and buy a newspaper from me. I knew that he received a newspaper at home, but he bought one from me anyhow. He then spent a few minutes just talking and sharing with me, telling me he was thinking about me and praying for me. Since my father died when I was seven months of age, the teacher became a father figure to me. He showed me that God loved me and wasn't too busy to be interested in Charles Stanley. He was a great encourager of my heart, and he probably was the one man who gave me the most balanced view of what God was like, a God of loving concern, a Friend not in a big hurry Who loved me and accepted me unconditionally.

Patient or Intolerant Teacher

Let's say you've blown it. You have pulled a boner, and you go before the Lord to talk about it. Is this what you hear Him say? "I understand. Let Me show you where you went wrong. Let Me show you why you didn't make it and why you're disappointed. Allow Me to show you exactly why you've become discouraged and how you can avoid it the next time around. Even if you do it again, though, I'm going to keep on loving you, because you've been accepted by grace not by behavior. I will teach you by My Spirit, even though you may stumble and fall, because My ultimate goal is that you become the person I want you to be, conformed to the image of My Son. So hang in there, because I'm going to always be with you."

Or is this the response you hear? "Well, you blew it again. Can't you get it through your thick skull that when I tell you something, that's the way I want it done? Why is it that I've told you the same thing over and over, and you continually make a mess out of things?"

If we see God as a patient Teacher who understands where we came from and how little we know, who understands that our family members were not practicing Christians, who understands our feelings of inferiority, then we will hear with an open, teachable heart.

If, however, we see God as a critical teacher who is always harping at our lack of spiritual understanding, then we will continually be waiting to be punished by this intolerant teacher who cannot stand our mistakes or failures. If that is our idea of God, then we are hearing a prefabricated, preprogrammed deity that did not originate from Scripture.

Often one of the reasons that our viewpoint of God is incorrect is that every time we go to church, turn on the television, or even read a book, someone is telling us, "You are sinning against God." "You are not obeying God." "You are not doing this." "You ought to do that." "God's displeased." "God's angry." We receive a verbal, emotional beating at every turn, and that is *not* in accordance with the biblical God. The God of the Bible is One whom we can come to and meet with patient understanding. He isn't critical, strict, and uncompromising. He doesn't scold us and make us feel inconsequential because we don't measure up.

Gentle or Angry Guide

We all have times in our lives when we get off course.

We take detours. We decide *that* is the path to pursue, but sometimes the result is debilitating. How does God respond?

Scripture says that in such a situation, God's response would be something like this: "Hold it now, Charles. You're off track. Let Me show you what's going to happen if you keep pursuing this matter. Let Me reveal to you how you can return to the proper course so as to avoid unfortunate consequences in the future."

Though He may chastise us to get us back on track, nowhere in the Bible does God say that He gets angry when one of His children strays. When we disobey Him, He doesn't get angry; He is grieved in His heart. The Holy Spirit within us tracks us down, reminding us of God's love and direction. The warning system begins to work, the lights begin to flash, telling us that we're out of the will of God, headed in the wrong direction.

He does not harshly remind us that we have once again made a poor decision. He doesn't pound us with our own inadequacy. That kind of outlook only makes us come to God condemned, guilty, and full of frustration, fears, and anxieties. Seeing Him in such a light puts us in bondage.

The negative side of all these attitudes toward God is one of the reasons the Church is weak today. We have the wrong viewpoint if we think of God as an angry guide. We don't understand Him, and we come to Him as beggars rather than as seekers in faith.

Understanding or Insensitive Counselor

When we talk to the Lord and bring our heartaches and fears to Him, what do we hear? Do we hear God saying, "That's okay. I understand how you feel. I know how you are hurting and why. I understand exactly why you blew it, and I want to tell you that I love you and I am going to help you."

Conversely, do we come to the Lord and say, "Lord, I hate to tell You this, but I'm really ashamed to come to You. I feel guilty and rather wicked about the whole thing. I've been to You so many times for forgiveness over this situation that I would perfectly understand if You don't allow me to come before You again. Please forgive me, God; please forgive me just this one more time."

When we unload the hurts of our spirits, the frustrations of our lives, God isn't the kind of Counselor who hurls back condemnation at us or piles guilt on top of us. Every person needs a counselor to whom the whole truth can be told, a counselor who won't retaliate angrily. If a worldly counselor can possess such compassion, certainly God can.

The kind of Counselor we as believers have is One from whom we cannot hide. He knows it all anyway, and we can tell Him anything we want to. In fact, we can tell Him how we feel about Him, even when the feelings aren't necessarily noble ones. No matter what we say, God still loves us, and as an understanding Counselor, He can take anything we give and accept us unconditionally. This understanding Counselor puts His arms around us and says, "That's okay." In fact, probably the most precious thing any counselor says to a broken, disillusioned heart is, "Everything's going to be all right." Is that the kind of Counselor we approach, or do we come to an insensitive counselor who is rather annoyed with our problems? Do we come filled with rejection because our behavior hasn't matched what is expected of us? Are this counselor's standards holiness and justice, without any compassion?

Most of us have experienced a severe time of grief. Wasn't the one who comforted you the most that individual who simply sat quietly with you? Wasn't the most effective minister the person who said little but wept with you and empathized with your hurt? The compassionate heart is the heart of God.

When Jesus healed and fed the multitudes, the Bible says He "was moved with compassion for them" (Matt. 9:36). When Christ looked out over Jerusalem, "He saw the city and wept over it" (Luke 19:41). David wrote in Psalm 103:8, "The LORD is merciful and gracious, Slow to anger, and abounding in mercy."

Generous or Reluctant Provider

When we bring our petitions before the Lord, do we hear a Father who says He delights in generously giving us all His riches in glory? Do we hear a God who says He delights in providing His children abundant and enjoyable treasures? Or do we encounter a God who is a reluctant provider, tabulating our requests on a spiritual calculator? Do we envision a God with a scratch pad out, keeping count of exactly how much He will divvy out to us this time?

The God of the Bible is not a calculating God. He is interested in blessing us with the maximum in our lives. That's why He promises that some believers will bring forth fruit 100-fold. That's not what I call a reluctant provider. An idea of a chintzy, somewhat tight-fisted God is a total misconception of the one, true, living God. If we come to God with a financial need and do not see Him as a generous Provider, we have two strikes against us. Our faith is already faltering, and we will have a problem receiving His blessing. All we will ask for is what we think we deserve, when in fact we don't deserve anything. That has nothing to do with it. We are to come asking God to bless us out of His infinite resources of grace, love, and mercy. The fact that we can come boldly to the Lord is emphasized in the story of the prodigal son (see Luke 15:11-32). There we see the portrait of a God who is ready and willing to bless His children with wonderful things. If we know God, we're not lost or prodigals; we are children of the King. We do not see Him as a stingy provider but as a generous one; we expect His goodness to permeate us.

If we come to God as spendthrifts, calculating just how much He can bless us with, then we will not receive the superabundant blessings of God, because we do not come in faith, we come in doubt. If we have a wrong perspective of God, we hear the wrong message.

Faithful or Inconsistent Sustainer

Almighty God is on our team. He is our faithful Sustainer. When everybody else abandons us, we can count on Him. When nobody else is willing to endure with us, He is there. He is trustworthy, reliable, and consistent. We can depend upon Him.

When we come to Him and ask for some support, we hear Him reply, "I'm right in there with you. Just endure in My love and grace and all of My omnipotence and omniscience is at your disposal. We are in this thing together. You have My strength." Or, when we pray, do we ask, "Lord, are you there? Lord, I just don't seem to hear anything from you. Why don't You talk or say anything to me, Lord?" Well, that's the wrong God, because the Scripture says that God's mercies are new or faithful every morning (see Lam. 3:23). Whether we get up at morning or midnight, His tender mercies are there waiting for us. We don't have to come to Him wondering if we are saying the right thing. We just come, knowing He is on our side and thanking Him that He is behind us all the way.

OUR ATTITUDE TOWARD HIM

If we come to God as rebellious, indifferent, and proud, we will not hear what He wants to convey. In order to hear, we must possess the right attitude toward God.

First of all, our attitude must be submissive. We need to come before the Lord and be willing to humble ourselves to do His will. We must be agreeable to tackling whatever tasks He has in mind.

Second, our attitude must be trusting. We must be absolutely convinced that God is going to lead us in the right direction and be confidently assured that He will guide us in the path of righteousness. We can never become fully intimate with a God we do not completely trust. Trusting God means acknowledging that He is totally and absolutely trustworthy.

Third, our attitude must be thankful. Even if yesterday was a disaster, we are to enter God's gates with thanksgiving and His courts with praise today.

What About Sin?

You might be wondering where sin fits in. Here is how it meshes with our attitude about God. When we willfully or impulsively sin against God, we still have a loving Father. We still have an intimate Friend. We still have a patient Teacher. We still have a gentle Guide, an understanding Counselor, a generous Provider, a faithful Sustainer.

Don't misunderstand. That's not getting by with sin. The God of the Bible who responds to our sin does not respond by trying to destroy us. Does a loving father destroy his child who misbehaves? Does he throw him out of the house? Of course not. Does an intimate friend turn his back when we break his trust? Does a patient teacher become increasingly angry when we have failed? Does a gentle guide become hostile when we lose our direction? Does an understanding counselor hurl animosities at us when we make mistakes? Does a generous provider or faithful sustainer cease to be benevolent when we're afraid to ask anymore? Too many people have negative ideas about God, and as a result, they are in emotional and spiritual imprisonment. That's why the Church is not a mighty army. That's why we're not excited about Jesus Christ and why we do not glorify God to the fullest measure. That's why we fail to share the message of Jesus Christ with boldness and confidence, because we are scared to death of God.

We do not hear the truth; therefore, we do not live in the truth. Now, I'm not belittling sin or its effects. A loving father is going to chastise a disobedient son, but he will do it in a spirit of love. A patient teacher will make the child stay after school until he learns, but the teacher will still be understanding. A gentle guide will put a wayward climber back on the right path, but the guide won't hurl him off the mountainside to do it!

Knowing that God is speaking is not enough. We must understand the character of the God we serve if we are to carry out His orders. Our relationship with Him, our understanding of Him, and our attitude toward Him all influence the content of His revelation to us.

Distortions of any of these factors will logically alter the substance of His communication. When they are in harmony with the scriptural principles, we can rest on the certainty of what we hear, for we listen to the One with whom there is "no shadow of turning" (see James 1:17).

CHAPTER SIX

Are You Listening?

SAMUEL WAS ONE of the mightiest prophets of the Old Testament. As I mentioned earlier, it's no coincidence that his first assignment from God necessitated that he learn how to hear God's Voice. In 1 Samuel 3:4–10, Samuel, who had been entrusted to the care of Eli the Priest, was lying down one evening when the Lord spoke:

> The LORD called Samuel. And he answered, "Here I am!" So he ran to Eli and said, "Here I am, for you called me." And he said, "I did not call; lie down again." And he [Samuel] went and lay down. And the LORD called yet again, "Samuel!" So Samuel arose and went to Eli, and said, "Here I am, for you called me." And he [Eli] answered, "I did not call, my son; lie down again." (Now Samuel did not yet know the LORD, nor was the word of the LORD yet revealed to him.) And the LORD called Samuel again the third time. Then he arose and went to Eli, and said, "Here I am, for you did call me." Then Eli perceived that the LORD had called the boy. Therefore Eli said to Samuel, "Go, lie down; and it shall be, if He calls you, that you must say, 'Speak, LORD, for Your servant hears.' " So Samuel went and lay down in his place. Then the LORD came and stood and called as at other times, "Samuel! Samuel!" And Samuel answered, "Speak, for Your servant hears."

Isn't that a beautiful way to answer God, "Speak, for Your servant hears." Eli taught Samuel how to listen to God, and if we are going to be men and women of God today, we must learn how we can hear what God is saying to us. We do so in a number of ways that I will discuss briefly here.

EXPECTANTLY

If we are going to listen to God, we must come to Him expectantly. We must anticipate His speaking to us. Jeremiah 33:3 exemplifies this eagerness when it quotes God, "Call to Me, and I will answer you, and show you great and mighty things, which you do not know." Throughout Scripture we have the promise that God will indeed speak to us, but if we come to Him doubting His ability to speak, we will have a difficult time listening. Expectantly believing the promises of God is expressing faith, without which "it is impossible to please Him" (see Heb. 11:6). We should all have great expectations when it comes to hearing Jehovah speak.

Expectancy is based on reliability. When Elijah confronted the 450 prophets of Baal and the 400 prophets of the Asherah, he did so with a boldness that seemed to border on downright insolence. After mocking the false prophets who were unable to call down fire from heaven to consume the prepared sacrifice of oxen, Elijah took his turn. You can almost imagine the smug grin on his face as he readied himself to call upon the God of Israel.

Before he did so, however, he had someone pour four large pitchers of water on the wood and oxen. For good measure, he had them drench the wood with four more pitchers, and just in case anyone thought it wasn't wet enough, he added another four, so that the "water ran all around the altar; and he also filled the trench with water" (1 Kings 18:35). Was he expecting God to answer?

You bet he was. He knew who the living, true God was because he had already seen God predict and execute drought. He had already witnessed His power at work in bringing the widow of Zarephath's son back to life. He had seen God's provision for her in supernaturally replenishing the bowl of flour and the jar of oil.

Elijah expected God to answer because He had faithfully responded in the past. Elijah's God is also our God, and His reliability hasn't altered one iota.

QUIETLY

The psalmist said, "Be still, and know that I am God" (Ps. 46:10). If we are to listen to God, we must be quiet and let Him do the talking. Too many of us, when we pray, simply read off a list of requests, get up, and walk off. Instead of listening to God, we only report our requests to Him. How can God speak to us if we don't take time to listen? Quietness is essential to listening. If we are too busy to listen, we won't hear. If we spend night after night watching television, and then try to listen, we will find our minds jammed with carnal interference. It takes time and quietness to prepare to listen to God. "My soul, wait silently for God alone, For my expectation is from Him" (Ps. 62:5).

That is why so many people through the centuries have sought seclusion in the deserts, mountains, or monasteries. There the noise of civilization vanishes and the Voice of God doesn't have quite so much competition. Such silence, however, can be found in the quiet of a living-room sofa late at night or at the kitchen table early in the morning. The place isn't important. The decibel scale is. God's Voice is still and quiet and easily buried under an avalanche of clamor.

PATIENTLY

God will not tell us some things instantaneously. We will hear some special revelations only after having waited a season of time. One of the reasons is simply that we're not always ready. Because of that, God will sometimes withhold information until we are prepared to listen.

We must be willing to listen to Him patiently, because these times may draw out and stretch our faith. He has promised to speak to our hearts, so we can expect Him to, but He is not compelled to tell us everything we want to know the moment we desire the information.

We'd like to say, "Lord, here's my order today. Please give me an answer before I get up off my knees." It may be weeks later before God speaks to us about this, not because He has forgotten, but because in the process of waiting, He is changing and preparing us to hear His message, which we may not have received had He spoken instantaneously.

ACTIVELY

To hear God we must actively wait and meditate upon His Word. Colossians 3:16 declares, "Let the word of Christ dwell in you richly in all wisdom, teaching and admonishing one another in psalms and hymns and spiritual songs, singing with grace in your hearts to the Lord."

If we only know the Word selectively and dwell on one

particular favorite subject, we fail to seek the whole counsel of God. The way we become wealthy and overflowing with the truth of the Word is to meditate upon Scripture, search it out, digest it, and apply it to our hearts.

Faced with one of the most difficult decisions in my life, I asked God to speak to my fearful, doubting heart. I was reading chapter 41 in the book of Isaiah when I came to the latter part of verse 9, and it was as if God said, "Now, Charles, 'You are My Servant, I have chosen you and have not cast you away: Fear not, for I am with you; Be not dismayed, for I am your God. I will strengthen you, Yes, I will help you, I will uphold you with My righteous right hand' " (vv. 9–10). I meditated upon that passage day and night for weeks, continually being reminded of His call to fearlessness and His assurance of divine help. "For I, the LORD your God, will hold your right hand, Saying to you, 'Fear not, I will help you' " (v. 13).

When the moment of crisis came, I was filled with an awesome sense of peace. That passage had permeated my very being. I felt that I was seeing my situation from God's viewpoint, relying upon His promise and His power to perform it. Once again I understood what Paul meant by the peace that surpasses all understanding.

At another time in my life, the Lord had brought me back to Psalm 81 in my morning meditation for several weeks. Verse 6 kept grabbing my attention: "I removed his shoulder from the burden; His hands were freed from the baskets." I knew God was trying to speak to me through that passage, but I was not sure what He was saying. The more I read and meditated, the more I began to realize that He was preparing me for a change. At the time, I was pastor of a large church in a big city. We had a

Christian school, which was growing rapidly, and I was heavily burdened because so much of the responsibility for it rested upon me.

After I spent several weeks meditating upon that passage and claiming it as a promise of relief, the Lord sent me a staff member who literally removed my shoulder from the burden and freed my hands from the baskets. She assumed the full responsibility of the school, and I was free to give my time to the church.

God is so precise in His instructions and promises given through His Word. Meditation upon God's Word is one of the most wonderful ways we can listen to the Voice of God for divine guidance.

CONFIDENTLY

We must be confident that when we listen to God, we will hear what we need to hear. It may not always be what we wish to hear, but God communicates to us what is essential in our walk with Him.

Would we withhold information from our children that they would need to possess in order to be obedient to our instructions? Would we tell them, "Here's what I want you to do," and then not provide them with information? Certainly not. The Lord Jesus said, "If you then, being evil, know how to give good gifts to your children, how much more will your Father who is in heaven give good things to those who ask Him!" (Matt. 7:11).

DEPENDENTLY

As we come to God, we must come in recognition that we are totally dependent upon the Holy Spirit to teach us truth. If we come to Him with a prideful attitude, it will be difficult for the Holy Spirit to instruct us. In 1 Corinthians 2:7–11 Paul wrote:

> But we speak the wisdom of God in a mystery, the hidden wisdom which God ordained before the ages for our glory, which none of the rulers of this age knew; for had they known, they would not have crucified the Lord of glory. But as it is written:
>
> *"Eye has not seen, nor ear heard,*
> *Nor have entered into the heart of man*
> *The things which God has prepared for*
> *those who love Him."*
>
> But God has revealed them to us through His Spirit. For the Spirit searches all things, yes, the deep things of God. For what man knows the things of a man except the spirit of the man which is in him? Even so no one knows the things of God except the Spirit of God.

There's no way for us to hear from God apart from the ministry of the Holy Spirit. When God speaks through others or through circumstances, it is the work of the Spirit.

Jesus said in John 16:7, "Nevertheless I tell you the truth. It is to your advantage that I go away; for if I do not go away, the Helper will not come to you; but if I depart, I will send Him to you." And in John 16:13 Christ explains, "For He [the Spirit] will not speak on His own authority, but whatever He hears He will speak; and He will tell you things to come."

We each have a living, divine receiver within us in the person of the Holy Spirit. That is why Paul added in 1 Corinthians 2:12, "Now we have received, not the spirit of the world, but the Spirit who is from God, that we might know the things that have been freely given to us by God." Prayer isn't God up there and us down here; it is the Holy Spirit speaking within us, bearing witness to our spirits that we may know the mind of Christ. In fact, we do have the mind of Christ, but how do we appropriate that for ourselves at any given moment? By receiving at that moment, by faith, that the Holy Spirit living within us will answer our petitions, speak to our hearts, and give us directions.

To receive God's directions we must have a right relationship with Him. That relationship means that we must be filled with His Spirit, and we must learn to walk in His Spirit, not grieving the Holy Spirit of God (see Eph. 4:30). If we grieve God by saying yes to sin and quench the Spirit by saying no to God, how can the Holy Spirit who is both receiver and communicator to our spirits declare God's revelation? One of the primary reasons people do not hear anything when they talk to God is because they are not living in the Spirit. Their life-style is one of quiet rebellion against God.

One of the reasons God commands us to be filled with the Spirit is that He not only empowers us for service but also is essential to our hearing God. If the Spirit is quenched and grieved, He cannot deliver the message of God because we are not listening. If we refuse to hear what the Holy Spirit says to us, then our praying is useless babbling into heaven and God does not hear it. How we live makes a difference as to what we hear. A believer can live what most would characterize as a normal Christian life and still be in error, because he is not listening to the Spirit. We can never get enough education, enough experience, to live independently of the Holy Spirit. He must give us the mind of Christ, or we do not possess it. He is not going to speak until we admit that apart from His genuine work in our lives, we are helpless to receive anything from Him.

We cannot make God tell us anything one split second before He is ready. We can fast and pray and weep and give, but that doesn't impress Him at all. The only way is to come humbly before Him, dependent upon the abiding, effective work of the Holy Spirit within us.

OPENLY

We must come to God openly. Second Timothy 3:16 is a familiar passage in which Paul wrote, "All Scripture is given by inspiration of God, and is profitable for doctrine, for reproof, for correction, for instruction in righteousness."

To listen openly means to be willing to hear God correct us as well as comfort us, to hear God convict us as well as assure us. We may be looking for a word of comfort from God when He may have a word of correction. If we come to Him only for comfort and prosperity, only for what is soothing to the ear, then we will not always hear what God has to say.

If we are unwilling to hear the correction, before long our need for correction will dramatically increase. As we listen to Him, humbly depending upon the Holy Spirit, God will bring to our minds areas that need to be corrected. We must accept both the positive and the negative.

Many of us have gotten on our knees before God and He spoke to us, but He didn't say what we wanted to hear. Even in the correction God has a positive goal in mind, and that is to prevent us from making disastrous mistakes and ruining our lives. When we come to Him with a mental spiritual sifter, picking out only what we want to hear, we will not hear accurately.

ATTENTIVELY

Listening to God demands our full attention. If He speaks through His Word (through His Spirit, through others, and through circumstances), then we must live every day attentively and alertly.

Someone might say something in passing that gives us a godly warning or admonition. God intended for it to drop into our spirits, nurture the truth, and bring it to life, letting it bud and blossom into correction and comfort. However, we must be attentive to produce such spiritual fruit. We must have our spiritual antennas fully extended. We must be vigilant to discern the Voice of God in the circumstances in our lives each day. We must constantly ask, "What is really happening? What does this particular circumstance mean?" As Christians we cannot divide our lives into secular and spiritual compartments. Our whole walk is spiritual because Christ is life. Of course not everything we do, think, or say is spiritual, but our walk is spiritual because we are new creations in Christ Jesus. Thus in everything God allows in our lives, we must always look for His fingerprint. We must listen for the Voice of God in every sound.

CAREFULLY

Hebrews 4:12 tells us about the power of the Word. It says, "For the word of God is living and powerful, and sharper than any two-edged sword, piercing even to the division of soul and spirit, and of joints and marrow, and is a discerner of the thoughts and intents of the heart."

In this verse, God informs us that everything we hear is to be sifted through the Word. Before we accept anything into our lives, we should filter it through Scripture and eliminate anything that contradicts Scripture. If it is contrary to the Word of God, it should be purged. That is why we must listen to Him carefully, because the Word of God reveals the innermost intentions and motivations of our lives. The Word of God pulls back the veil so that we can see the reality of all that is about us. The light of the Word illuminates everything enabling us to discern the truth from error. Whatever we hear we must thoroughly check out against the absolute standard of His truth.

SUBMISSIVELY

We need to listen to God submissively, because sometimes when He speaks to our hearts, we will not like what we hear. When the Lord tells us something we don't want to hear, we may not react in total obedience. But God doesn't get hostile over our rebellious spirits, that's not His response. He knew us before we ever came to listen to Him, and He knew exactly how we would respond. He may be grieved by our negative reaction, but He doesn't send down a squadron of angry angels to destroy us. He knows we will struggle with certain things.

When Jesus came to the Garden of Gethsemane, He was already committed to the Father's will. However, He struggled with the Father to determine whether there was another way to accomplish God's purpose. He struggled with separation from the Father while at the same time He was committed to God's will. There will be times when we come to God, listen to Him, and then grapple with what we hear. We may not be consistently disobedient to what we hear, but sometimes we may not understand how or why God is going to perform it. We may be as submissive as we know how at that moment, but still wrestle with what He says. Submission must ultimately accompany listening if we are to fully hear God. It is essential if we are to follow Him.

I recall a man who had just come out of the air force after World War II. He had been a skilled flight instructor and was expecting to join a major airline and spend the rest of his life as a commercial pilot. It would have been a good-paying job and one where, he felt, he could be a witness for Christ.

The Lord had other ideas. As he pondered several offers, the man was asked by a longtime friend to join him in evangelism work. He didn't like the idea and told God so. When the time came to give an answer to the airlines, however, he declined and went into full-time ministry, where he successfully labored for thirty years.

He told me there were many times when he watched jets fly overhead and he dreamed of piloting. He continued to receive lucrative offers to return to flying, but he turned them all down because he wanted to be submissive to God. Because of that yieldedness, he accomplished God's purpose in life, walking in the works He had ordained, not in his own well-laid scheme.

GRATEFULLY

When we come to the Father, we should have a grateful attitude. We should be grateful the Father would love us enough to send His only begotten Son to the cross; grateful for the crucifixion; grateful for our salvation; grateful that God has plucked us out of the kingdom of darkness and put us into the kingdom of light. As Paul explained in Philippians 4:6 and 7, "Be anxious for nothing, but in everything by prayer and supplication, with thanksgiving, let your requests be made known to God; and the peace of God, which surpasses all understanding, will guard your hearts and minds through Christ Jesus."

Out of the billions of people who make up this universe, God is interested in you. He possesses intimate knowledge of you in His incomparable, indescribable mind. When you come to Him, you should draw near with a thankful heart, because you do not come in contact with a heavenly Father who speaks to the masses, but one who speaks to individuals. That should invoke your unlimited gratitude.

REVERENTLY

A reverent heart should be the foundation of hearing God. We should be in awe that we can speak to the God who hung the sun and world on nothing, the God who created all the intricacies of human life.

We should be humble that this same omnipotent God is quietly willing to listen to us, while simultaneously giving direction to the vastness of the universe. His total, concentrated and undisturbed attention is focused upon us individually. That ought to humble us and create within us a reverence that acknowledges God for the mighty Creator He is.

CHAPTER SEVEN

Sitting Before the Lord

JUST THE MENTION of the word *meditation* conjures up various and sundry images, all somewhat foreign to the Western mind. Somehow or another, contemporary believers have removed the word from the biblical vocabulary. Its usage now has been confined primarily to the practice of Eastern religion and, thus for the Christian, cast into an almost obsolete and forbidden sphere. This abandonment is at our great peril, because meditation and its scriptural application are of immense value if we are to listen accurately to God.

Perhaps no other man has pursued this godly endeavor more fervently and fruitfully than King David. Many of the psalms are the results of his quietly waiting and reflecting upon God. As a "man after God's own heart," David first had to know the mind and heart of God. To a large extent, David accomplished this through the persistent practice of godly meditation. A vivid illustration can be found in 2 Samuel 7. In this chapter we see that David has reached a place of rest in his reign. His war campaigns are no longer on the drawing board, and he is now contemplating building a temple for the Lord. The prophet Nathan gives an encouraging message of God's faithfulness to David and the Lord's plan for constructing the temple. David's response to Nathan's communiqué is found in 2 Samuel 7:18, "Then King David went in and sat before the LORD; and he said: 'Who am I, O Lord GOD? And what is my house, that You have brought me this far?' " Notice the phrase, David "sat before the LORD." Now he wasn't sitting in a chair as we would. He was kneeling and sitting back on his heels, listening, and talking to the Lord. David was meditating.

In his book, *Knowing God*, author J. I. Packer gives as good a working definition of meditation as I have seen:

> Meditation is the activity of calling to mind, and think-ing over, and dwelling on, and applying to oneself, the var-ious things that one knows about the works and ways and purposes and promises of God. It is an activity of holy thought, consciously performed in the presence of God, under the eye of God, by the help of God as a means of communion with God. Its purpose is to clear one's mental and spiritual vision of God, and to let His truth make its full and proper impact on one's mind and heart. It is a mat-ter of talking to oneself about God and oneself; it is, in-deed, often a matter of arguing with oneself, reasoning oneself out of moods of doubt and unbelief into a clear ap-prehension of God's power and grace. Its effect is to ever humble us as we contemplate God's greatness and glory, and our own littleness and sinfulness and to encourage and reassure us—"comfort" us in the old, strong Bible sense of the word—as we contemplate the unsearchable riches of divine mercy displayed in the Lord Jesus Christ.

Meditation was nothing new to David because he had long known what it meant to meditate. We read in the Psalms how often he listened and talked to the Father out in the fields. Even when he was running from Saul and dodging javelins, David took time to meditate upon God.

Since meditation is the one activity that should be the

daily priority of believers, it is the one discipline Satan will doggedly keep us from observing. When we examine the rewards and the results of meditation, however, we will soon realize it can't be secondary. It has to be primary.

Many believers think that meditation is only for ministers or other spiritual leaders. They do not see its role in a secular world where strife and competition reign. It seems alien to persons who have to get up and hit the expressway at 7:30 A.M., be in noisy offices during the day, and then battle the traffic home, where they then must deal with domestic difficulties. Yet it is in the midst of such constant turmoil that the believer stands in great need of the quieting effects of meditation, so that he may distill God's Voice from the roar of everyday living. God gave the practice of meditation not just to preachers, but to all His children so that we might better relate to Him. Personal, private meditation begins when we get alone with the Lord and get quiet before Him. It may be for five minutes, it may be for thirty minutes, it may be for an hour. The important thing is that we get alone with the Lord to find His direction and purpose for our lives.

Personal and compelling guidance is only one of the benefits of meditation. Psalm 119:97–100 lists some of the other rewards of meditation, such as wisdom, discernment, keen insight, and heightened obedience.

Joshua 1:8 is a wonderful Scripture on the blessed benefits of concentrated thinking. "This Book of the Law shall not depart from your mouth, but you shall meditate in it day and night, that you may observe to do according to all that is written in it. For then you will make your way prosperous, and then you will have good success." Meditation is God's way of crowning our lives with His success and prosperity of soul, spirit, and body. It is also a catalyst to obedient living.

I want to share four principles that will guide you into meaningful meditation. These principles will be liberating truths that will cause you to hear the Voice of God in a fresh, invigorating manner.

REVIEW THE PAST

Reviewing the past is an excellent way to begin our time of meditation, because as we do, we will see patterns that God has woven into our lives. One of the first steps that David took in 2 Samuel 7:18 was to recall God's blessings, "Who am I, O Lord GOD? And what is my house, that You have brought me this far?" David remembered his fight with Goliath. He remembered the years spent running from Saul, the battles he had won. Now that he had peace in his life, he had the privilege of savoring God's wonderful works.

When we meditate, we should focus on how God has operated in our lives in the past. We should look for His hand in all of our dealings. As we do, we can see His hand of correction, comfort, and exhortation, and we can better distinguish His moving in our lives at the present time.

REFLECT UPON GOD

Reviewing the past should be followed by reflecting upon God. Listen to what else David said: "And yet this was a small thing in Your sight, O Lord GOD....Now what more can David say to You? For You, Lord GOD, know Your servant. For Your Word's sake, and according to Your own heart, You have done all these great things, to make Your servant know them" (2 Sam. 7:19–21).

As we begin to reflect upon God, we should consider three facets: first, His *greatness*; second, His *grace*; and third, His *goodness*. When we meditate on the greatness of God and His names—Jehovah, Yahweh, Elohim, Everlasting, Infinite in Power, Absolute in Faithfulness—our gigantic mountains of trouble and heartache shrink in comparison. In the light of the presence and greatness of God, nothing is impossible in our lives. Our burdens dissipate in His very presence.

Focusing on difficulties intensifies and enlarges the problem. When we focus our attention on God, the problem is put into its proper perspective, and it no longer overwhelms us.

Jeremiah Denton was a prisoner of war in North Vietnam for seven horrendous years. As one of the highest ranking American captives, he was subjected to particularly grueling torture, spending almost his entire incarceration in solitary confinement. In such a barren, brutal situation, it would be hard not to focus on the pain and tedium. Yet, Denton not only survived but also came back and was elected a United States senator from Alabama.

How did he survive? He stated on many occasions that an essential survival skill was quoting passages from the Bible. Internalized Scripture became the unseen sword that enabled him to fend off the cruelest weapons of the enemy. By inwardly focusing on the power of God to sustain and strengthen him, he was able to rise above the squalor of his lonely existence.

REMEMBER GOD'S PROMISES

As David continued to meditate on the Lord, he said: "And now, O Lord GOD, You are God, and Your words are true, and You have promised this goodness to Your servant" (2 Sam. 7:28). David recalled God's promises in establishing his name and family on an everlasting basis. When we kneel or sit before God and meditate upon Him, it's beneficial to review His mighty promises.

In Scripture, He has promised us peace, He has promised us provision, He has promised us protection. These promises belong to each of His children. When we meditate upon God and remember the promises He has given us in His Word, our faith grows and our fears dissolve. David understood that. Many times, in the caves hiding from Saul and with from six to twenty thousand men searching for him, David quietly shifted his attention to God. Under the stars or in the darkness of the caves, David focused his attention on God who had equipped him to slay Goliath, who had given him swiftness of body and keenness of mind. He remembered God who had allowed him to avoid the penetrating point of Saul's javelin. As he fixed his inner man upon God, his fears and frustrations were soothed by the presence of God.

MAKE A REQUEST

As we sit before the Lord in meditation, we shouldn't just listen; there is a time to make a request too. In 2 Samuel 7:29 David asked, "Now therefore, let it please You to bless the house of Your servant, that it may continue forever before You." What a tremendous request! He doesn't just ask God to bless his family; he boldly asks God's everlasting favor. And God answered his prayer.

On one occasion I was meditating upon the Word, and I came to Philippians 4:19: "And my God shall supply all your need according to His riches in glory by Christ Jesus." Suddenly I stopped. I began to meditate upon that verse. Without previous thought upon the subject, I prayed for God to provide a large sum of money. I didn't even have a purpose for it. I was burdened to ask for it and to expect it. Several days went by and my burden grew heavier, and all the time I wondered why. Without warning, I had a rather large financial need. Within a matter of hours, God supplied the finances to meet that need. He had burdened me to ask even before I knew I had a need! He had already set in motion to supply a need I didn't even know would exist.

REQUIREMENTS FOR MEDITATION

If we are to have a profitable time of meditation, we can't just rush in, jot down one or two prayer requests, quickly pray, and then go on to dinner. That's not what God wants. He wants us to sit before Him.

Meditation isn't a spontaneous occurrence. Certain disciplines must be put in play in order for us to receive the full benefits of its application. Certain requirements must be heeded if the biblical practice of meditation is to be more than just wishful thinking.

These are the principles that have aided me in personal meditation.

A Season of Time

When we think about meditating on the Lord, the first requirement is a season of time. The length of time, whether it's five minutes or an hour, will be determined by our purpose. If we are in deep distress about a subject, the period will be lengthened. If we simply want to be quiet, it may be a matter of minutes. Psalm 62:5 enjoins us to "wait silently for God alone, For my expectation is from Him."

When we tell God we don't have time for Him, we are really saying we don't have time for life, for joy, for peace, for direction, for prosperity, because He is the source of all these. The essence of meditation is a period of time set aside to contemplate the Lord, listen to Him, and allow Him to permeate our spirits. When we do, something happens within us that equips us to carry out our duties, whether as a mother, a clerk, a secretary, a mechanic, a carpenter, a lawyer. Whatever we do, the time of meditation is God's time of equipping us in preparation for life.

It is amazing what God can do to a troubled heart in a short period of time, when that person understands the meaning of meditation. We live in a hurried and rushed world, and it's not going to slow down. So each of us must ask, "How am I going to stay in the rush of it all and hear God?" I'm convinced that the man who has learned to meditate upon the Lord will be able to run on his feet and walk in his spirit. Although he may be hurried by his vocation, that's not the issue. The issue is how fast his spirit is going. To slow it down requires a period of time.

The most important lesson parents can teach their children is the practical importance of prayer and meditation. In doing so, they give their children a lifetime compass. When children learn early to listen to God and obey Him, and when they learn that He is interested in what interests them, they develop a sense of security that no other gift will give them. God is always available, no matter what the circumstances. He will always be there when parents are unavailable.

My wife and I used to pray before our children were ever born, "Lord show us how to teach our children to pray and listen to You." My heart rejoices as I see and hear them practicing that precious lesson.

The only way to teach your children to spend time with the Lord is by example. They need to hear you praying, walk in on you praying, listen to you share how God is speaking to you. They will soon realize that if God hears the prayers of Mom and Dad, He will hear theirs as well. You could not give your children a greater heritage than praying parents.

Stillness

If we're really going to meditate upon the Lord, stillness is a key. Psalm 46:10 says, "Be still, and know that I am God." We'll know God best when we not only set aside time for Him but also learn to be still before Him.

Stillness brings us to the point where we can concentrate. It's difficult to fix our thoughts upon God as we barrel the expressway or stand in the midst of noisy friends. We often miss God's most beautiful interventions in our lives because we are so distracted by other things that we can't see or hear Him. We are not sensitive before Him. We haven't learned to be still in His presence.

When we become still before the Lord, gradually the competing elements of life ebb away. God's benevolent goodness, greatness, and grace come to the forefront of our minds and our problems begin to diminish.

Seclusion

Mark wrote of Jesus: "Now in the morning, having risen a long while before daylight, He went out and departed to a solitary place; and there He prayed" (Mark 1:35). If the Lord Jesus Christ, who was perfect in His relationship with the Father, felt it necessary to leave the twelve disciples whom He loved the most and seclude Himself before God, then shouldn't we make provisions for such solitude?

Everybody needs to be alone at times. It's wonderful for husbands and wives to love each other and to want to be together, but there are times when they need to be apart. When each one meditates in solitude before God, nothing will bring the couple closer to intimacy with each other.

God wants you alone sometimes because He wants your absolute, undivided attention. For example, suppose your spouse was always with four or five people twenty-four hours a day. It wouldn't take very long before you would grow rather annoyed at that problem. So, too, God wants you to have a private time with Him, free from the competition of others. He loves just plain, simple, exciting *you*. He wants you all to Himself to put His loving, divine arms around you.

God doesn't hug two people at a time; He hugs us one at a time. He loves us one at a time, but unless we are willing to get alone with Him, our minds will always be divided. Private meditation allows the Lord Jesus Christ to have each of us all to Himself. His private workings are often His most precious.

Silence

Oftentimes God wants us to sit before Him in quietness. He doesn't want us to do all the talking. As Isaiah 30:15 says: "In quiet and confidence shall be your strength."

For some people, meditation is best described as a one-way conversation. They have no real relationship with God because they do all the talking. To have God speak to the heart is a majestic experience, an experience these people may miss if they monopolize the conversation and never pause to hear God's responses.

If we quiet ourselves before Him, God can interject His thoughts into our thinking. If we are silent for a few moments, He may bring a favorite passage of Scripture to mind, He may reveal an absorbing truth, or He may bring peace to our inner beings—or He may do all three. We should sit before Him in silence and allow Him to pour Himself into us.

Silence and seclusion before God allow Him to speak to our hearts clearly, positively, and unmistakably. Though God may not speak to us audibly, He will move in our spirits and impress our minds. We will know God has spoken to us. God saved us to glorify Him, and He developed a relationship with us so that we can love and understand who He is.

Self-Control

When we meditate, we may feel as if nothing is happening outwardly. Just because we can't detect God's functioning overtly doesn't mean that God is not at work. Just as Paul had to learn to keep his body under control (see 1 Cor. 9:27), every believer should consider self-control a necessary discipline.

As we begin to meditate, we may have to labor mentally a bit to focus our attention on God. If that sometimes is a problem, we can turn to a psalm and say, "Lord, I have a hard time keeping my mind on the subject at hand. I want to get immersed in this psalm and get my attention on You."

In a few moments you can stop reading and begin to think just about Him. As you do, become lost in His grandeur. There can be nothing better, more productive, or more rewarding in your life than to become lost in great thoughts about a great God.

Proverbs 8:34 exclaims, "Blessed is the man who listens to me, Watching daily at my gates, Waiting at the posts of my doors." Notice the word *daily.* That means that the believer must take deliberate steps each day to bring his mind, body, and life under control so that he can spend time waiting and listening for God to speak.

Some people feel that certain body postures can aid in the practice of meditation. Others prefer to sit quietly with the palms of their hands raised upward to the heavens to receive gifts from above. Still others opt to kneel or even lie prostrate on the floor. I would encourage each individual to discover the posture he is most comfortable with, keeping in mind that God is, above all else, interested in the position of our hearts, not our bodies.

Submission

James wrote: "Humble yourselves in the sight of the Lord, and He will lift you up" (James 4:10). If we are rebellious in our hearts and insist on having our own way, we won't meditate. Rebellion is the antithesis of submission, and if we are to hear Him adequately, our minds and hearts must be totally surrendered to Him. Yieldedness is vital in listening to what He has to say.

When we refuse to deal with the problem God has pinpointed, we don't lose our standing with Him. We are still saved, our relationship is the same, but our enjoyment of His fellowship is broken. Do you suppose it is possible that the primary reason we don't spend more time alone with God is we don't want to face the certain type of music He keeps sending our way? It is a song which says, "Give up. Surrender. Yield. Let Me love you to the maximum of My potential, so that you will reach the maximum of your potential."

Now let's discover the rewards of spending time alone with God, thinking about Him, adoring Him, and praising Him.

A NEW PERSPECTIVE

When we meditate upon the Lord, we see things from a different perspective. The things that worry us lose their grip. The things that weaken us, God turns into strength. Our viewpoint of others and ourselves, of our tasks and our problems, even of our enemies changes because we see them from God's viewpoint. Our inward look at problems or situations is replaced by a heavenly view, because we learn that we are seated in the heavenly places in Christ Jesus. Meditation brings us to a position in which we can see ourselves in the light of God's truth.

David declared in Psalm 36:9: "In Your light we see light." There is something about having God shed His enlightenment on a subject that causes us to see clearly His truth. Paul prayed that the Ephesians might be given a "spirit of wisdom and revelation in the knowledge of Him" so that "the eyes of your understanding [may be] enlightened" (Eph. 1:17–18). We cannot rightly see ourselves or God without His revealing participation.

The pressures in our lives begin to dissipate when we are secluded, silent, and still before the Lord. God pulls the plug in the pressure tanks of our lives, and our anxieties begin to drain. When we first begin to meditate, our frustration levels are usually at full, but the longer we sit focusing upon Him, the emptier the reservoirs of tension become. Biblical meditation causes something to happen to our spirits, in our souls and our emotional beings, even in our human bodies. Our physical tiredness is somehow lessened. Isn't it strange that we will sit down to watch television for three to four hours a night, just to get relaxed, when the Divine Relaxer can do it in a few minutes? Focusing attention on God can help believers go to sleep, peaceful and relaxed, despite the difficulties of the day.

Peace

Jesus said, "My peace I give to you" (see John 14:27). Christ who lives within us comes to the forefront of our lives. He becomes the all in all.

A Positive Attitude

As God substitutes peace for pressure, a positive attitude replaces a negative one. We can't wait to get up the next morning to see what God is going to do in our lives. When we spend time with God, our old selfish selves move out of the way and let the radiant Christ within us blossom and grow.

Personal Intimacy

When we sit before the Lord, it's like the experience we had when we met that special person for the first time. As we talked and shared our hearts, our joys, and our hurts, we grew intimately interested in each other.

As time passed, we realized that we could live with that person for the rest of our lives. It's the same with God. He never wants us to think of Him as distant or detached. Through the Holy Spirit, God lives intimately with each of us. He is embedded within the deepest core of our lives, and He desires fellowship with us so that He can pour His life into us. But, He can't do that if we fail to spend time meditating upon Him and learning who He is.

Purification

As an expression of His love and devotion to us, God will often put His finger on areas of our lives that are conspicuously wrong. Because He loves us, He wants to cleanse us so that we might be filled with His life and joy.

That is when we either run away or develop our relationship with Him. When we are willing to sit before Him and let Him expose our hearts, something happens. He prunes from our lives what isn't clean. However, if we rationalize our problems when He points them out, we will spend less and less time meditating, because we won't want to face God in that area of our lives.

If we don't want to be alone with God, it may be because He is dealing with particular points in our lives that we simply don't want exposed. We will not let Him love us.

When two people who live together intimately have something wrong in their relationship, they don't really have to tell each other. Both of them know it. When we are quiet before the Lord, and He wants to do something in our lives and things are not right, we stymie our growth by not yielding to Him. We work against the very God who is on our side, working for us, encouraging us, building us up. So whatever He brings to mind, the best thing is to admit it, confess it, repent of it, and deal with it. That is the only way to keep the sweet fellowship of meditation.

Ongoing personal purification was one of the chief attributes that made David a man after God's own heart. We all know that he was far from perfect. His record as a murderer and adulterer would eliminate him from any pulpit in America, yet Jesus referred to Himself as the "Offspring of David" (see Rev. 22:16). How could David commit such gross iniquity and still obtain such divine affirmation?

I believe it was because David was zealous to confess and repent whenever God pinpointed David's sin and confronted him with it. Psalm 51 has been the soulful prayer of many a believer who has willfully or blindly offended God, as David's remorse was laid open before God.

When he wrongfully numbered the children of Israel in a census, he quickly admitted his wrongdoing. "And David's heart condemned him after he had numbered the people. So David said to the LORD, 'I have sinned greatly in what I have done; but now, I pray, O LORD, take away the iniquity of Your servant, for I have done very foolishly' " (2 Sam. 24:10). Rather than run from God's searching, probing light, David humbled himself before the Lord, confessing his transgressions and asking God to cleanse him.

A Passion for Obedience

As we kneel before God and He pours Himself into us, we in turn give ourselves in devotion to Him. The result is that God places within us a passion for obedience. We want to obey God. Nobody has to prod us. We don't have to hear sermons to make us obey Him. Obedience is now part of our inner beings.

We can be tired, weary, and emotionally distraught, but after spending time alone with God, we find that He injects into our bodies energy, power, and strength. God's spiritual dynamics are at work in our inner beings, refreshing and energizing our minds and spirits. There is nothing to match meditation in its impact upon our lives and the lives of others.

An unschooled man who knows how to meditate upon the Lord has learned far more than the man with the highest education who does not know how to meditate. Education not backed with meditation is doomed for failure. When we make time alone with Christ a priority of our lives, it affects and influences every single facet of our lives. Of all the things Christ wants for us, loving Him and focusing our attention on Him are the most important. Then we can follow Him and receive all He has prepared for us.

I am always moved when I read one special verse in the fourth chapter of Acts. Let me describe the situation leading up to it. Filled with the newly discovered power of the Holy Spirit, Peter and John have been ministering powerfully. Thousands have been saved and great numbers added to the fledgling group of Christians.

Peter and John were arrested by the Sadducees and brought before Annas the high priest, Caiaphas, John, and Alexander, all of high-priestly descent. They placed Peter and John squarely in the center of their contemporaries and asked about the nature of the disciples' work.

Picture it for a minute, won't you? Peter and John, two

large, cedar-rough fishermen with a minimum amount of education, stood before a room full of highly educated, influential, skilled, religious rulers.

The outcome of the confrontation is electrifying. Immediately, Peter took the offensive, pushing the Sadducees into the proverbial corner. He attacked with power and persuasiveness. His hearers were startled. Luke recorded their amazement in the potent language of Acts 4:13: "Now when they saw the boldness of Peter and John, and perceived that they were uneducated and untrained men, they marveled. And they realized that they had been with Jesus."

Though the rulers referred to the two men's association with Jesus, the principle holds true for us today. The amount of time we spend with Jesus—meditating on His Word and His majesty, seeking His face—establishes our fruitfulness in the kingdom. Meditation is simply a matter of spending our time in rich fellowship with our personal Lord and Savior. Do people recognize us as "having been with Jesus"?

CHAPTER EIGHT

Your Spiritual Mind-Set

JOHN AND JAMES sit next to each other in church every Sunday, and they listen to the same message. John is maturing in his faith and learning to walk in the Spirit. His life is productive and fruitful. Meanwhile, James is not growing; he does not share his faith, and he is not productive. How can this paradox be explained?

How can a husband and wife sit in the same pew, but one grows and one remains stagnant? How can two collegians hear the very same message or broadcast, or read the same book, but one comes away excited and the other totally unmotivated?

Could it be that we come to God with certain mindsets that determine our responses? Could it be that we are often mentally and spiritually predetermined to select what we want to listen to and ignore (at our own peril) what we need to hear?

A poem by Ella Wheeler Wilcox goes like this:

> One ship drives east and another drives west
> With the selfsame winds that blow.
> 'Tis the set of the sails
> And not the gales which tells us the way to go.

I am convinced that our spiritual mind-set in hearing and appropriating scriptural truth greatly affects how we listen to God. In Matthew 13:1-9, Jesus gave us a familiar parable that plainly illustrates four different types of spiritual hearers, who each heard the Word through different spiritual gifts.

> On the same day Jesus went out of the house and sat by the sea. And great multitudes were gathered together to Him, so that He got into a boat and sat; and the whole multitude stood on the shore. Then He spoke many things to them in parables, saying: "Behold, a sower went out to sow. And as he sowed, some seed fell by the wayside; and the birds came and devoured them. Some fell on stony places, where they did not have much earth; and they immediately sprang up because they had no depth of earth. But when the sun was up they were scorched, and because they had no root they withered away. And some fell among thorns, and the thorns sprang up and choked them. But others fell on good ground and yielded a crop: some a hundredfold, some sixty, some thirty. He who has ears to hear, let him hear!"

The type of sowing Jesus depicted in this parable involved a very narrow strip of soil cleaned of rock and thorny bushes. Adjacent to the strip were paths for donkeys and people. The people would scatter the seed as they walked, just as we would in our yards. Occasionally they would put a sack of seed on a donkey, cut a small hole in the sack, walk through the field, and let the seed drop out. Sometimes the wind would blow seeds on to unprepared soil, or the animal would randomly drop seeds as it crossed the hardened path alongside the rows.

A CLOSED MIND

In verse 4, Jesus said, "Some seed fell by the wayside; and the birds came and devoured them." Jesus' own interpretation of this is found in verse 19: "When anyone hears the word of the kingdom, and does not understand it, then the wicked one comes and snatches away what was sown in his heart. This is he who received seed by the wayside."

The first type of hearer is one with a closed mind. That doesn't mean just the unbeliever, because the believer can fit into this category too. We could be talking about a person who regularly goes to church or who frequently listens to gospel programs on television and radio. A close-minded person is one who decides what he is going to hear and what he is not going to hear. He shuts his mind to anything that demands of him something he does not choose to give.

Such people sit and listen passively. They have sat through hundreds of sermons but have no intention of applying what was said or of changing their behavior. Their minds are closed because they have so often heard the truth without responding; that is a dangerous position.

Their hearts become hardened when they grow passive in their listening, not taking the initiative to respond. When these people hear, it's like seed dropped on the hard surface where it has no chance of germinating. It lies for the animals and the people to trample on, baked dry in the sun.

Passive listeners will listen up to a point but then hedge their commitments. When their absolute obedience is commanded, their minds slam shut like a door in a stiff wind. Literally thousands of believers go to church with such a stubborn mind-set. Even before they arrive, they have already determined the limits of truth they will accept. They are willing to listen as long as what they hear doesn't get too personal. When the requirements about commitment to the lordship of Christ get too stringent, they become callous, because they have heard so often without obeying the truth. When that happens, Satan comes along and steals the truth. If they do not take the initiative to apply the truth they have heard, Satan will steal it out of their lives every time.

After all, why should God continue to allow them to hear one truth after the other when they are not going to do anything about it? To listen passively to Scripture, which is the eternal Word of the living God, is a sin against God. To prescribe arbitrarily areas that God can enter in their lives denies His lordship.

Unfortunately, when the bottom falls out in their lives and they cry out to a God whom they've refused to listen to for years, they have a difficult time talking to Him. It is not because God hasn't been listening all those years, but because of the callousness of their spirits.

People are actually better off never to hear God's Word than to attend church and listen passively, committed to a closed mind. God is going to touch every part of our lives whether we like it or not; He will deal with every minute aspect of our existence. The people who play the fool are the ones who callously listen to truth. They don't become callous by refusing to listen to God or by arguing with God; they become callous by listening and *not responding*.

For months I witnessed to an administrator at a nearby university. Occasionally he would attend the Sunday-morning service, but he always scoffed at anything miraculous or supernatural. His mind was closed. He attended only to please his wife.

One Sunday afternoon, he had invited friends to his

home for a cookout. A sudden cloudburst sent everyone hurrying into the house to escape the downpour. He was the last one to run for cover. With his hands full and body soaked, he ran toward the sliding glass door, not realizing that the last person through had closed it. He smashed through the glass. In a matter of seconds, he was lying in a pool of blood.

On my second visit with him in the hospital, he said to me, "I have been thinking about what you have been trying to tell me. I think I am now ready to listen." It took near-tragedy to get him to listen, but he did. He was saved and became a bold witness for the Lord.

There are multitudes who sit and listen, who read the gospel every week, but never think about what they encounter. They never sift through it in their lives. They never apply it. Their minds are closed.

A CLOUDY MIND

In verses 5 and 6 of the parable, Jesus described a second type of listener: "Some fell on stony places, where they did not have much earth; and they immediately sprang up because they had no depth of earth. But when the sun was up they were scorched, and because they had no root they withered away." In verses 20 and 21, Jesus interpreted the analogy: "But he who received the seed on stony places, this is he who hears the word and immediately receives it with joy; yet he has no root in himself, but endures only for a while. For when tribulation or persecution arises because of the word, immediately he stumbles."

Even when Palestinian farmers cleared out a section of land to plant their crops, only a thin layer of soil was on top of a rocky area, leaving the seed too little earth to take root in. As the plant sprouted in the hot sun, it withered away almost immediately. Depicted in this section of the parable is the hearer with the cloudy mind. Cloudy-minded hearers listen to the Word of God and get excited. They trust the Lord Jesus Christ as their Savior. Having been saved, they just want to praise the Lord and enjoy the thrill. The problem is, they don't take the time to study Scripture and sink their roots into the Word of God so they may gain a firm foundation; they are not attached to anything. They have no doctrinal basis. When the storms and the heat come they've had it.

This is why so many people who have been Christians for quite some time fall apart when they experience a crisis. They just rip apart at the seams. They shout, "Hallelujah!" until an affliction comes along and devastates them. Why? Because their minds are addled with confusion, turmoil, and unbelief. The lack of spiritual exercise has made their spirits and minds flabby and unable to respond to the urgency of the problem.

It's one thing to have an experience, but if we don't know what the foundation of that experience is, we're headed for trouble. We are to constantly renew our minds and ground ourselves in the Word of God. We should all be willing to examine ourselves and see if we really know *why* we believe what we believe. We should be able to tell others why we believe in the forgiveness of sin, why we're not afraid of dying, how our bodies will be resurrected, or what it means to be justified, redeemed, sanctified, and reconciled. Taking root means that we dig deep into the Word for ourselves and discover the firmness of His Word.

If our names are in the Lamb's Book of Life and we

hope to miss all of life's afflictions until we arrive in heaven, we're in serious trouble. Believers are going to be tried and tested in the fires of affliction. When we have no root in the truth, we simply can't take the heat.

The vacillating world of the adolescent is a good example of the cloudy mind. One day he struggles to act like a mature adult, and the next day he lapses into obvious juvenile behavior. He sways back and forth like a tree bending in the wind.

Such people are susceptible to the cults that come along because they are not firmly entrenched in the knowledge of the Word of God. They are prime targets for anybody who happens by with something new because they always want a new experience. They are not satisfied with Jesus because they do not know Him. If they would take the effort to dig in deeper into the Word of God, they would discover how exciting Jesus Christ really is.

Jesus Christ isn't a temporary, momentary thrill. He is life! If an individual is satisfied being saved and keeping a cloudy mind, and not knowing what he believes, why he believes, or *who* he believes in, then he is a poor listener. The cloudy-minded hearer has no real intention of investigating the Word or of growing. He just likes the security of missing hell and going to heaven.

Most of us have heard multitudes of sermons, but how much do we remember of them? Are we listening with cloudy minds, or are we listening for God to add another significant truth to our lives?

The cloudy-minded hearer risks the danger of relaying unsound faith to his offspring, although he may not do it intentionally. His instability in the Word is transmitted by example to impressionable children, who never really learn how to be firmly grounded in Scripture or belief. As a result, his children are prime targets for silver-tongued deceivers who undermine their weak biblical foundations with what seem to be convincing arguments.

The father who constantly analyzes the truth heard through church, Bible-study groups, or personal devotions encourages his family to sink its roots deep into the Word. The father who persistently seeks to teach his children how to apply the Word of God gives them a support system that will withstand the extreme storms of doubt and skepticism.

A CLUTTERED MIND

The third category of listener is pictured by Jesus in verse 7: "And some fell among thorns, and the thorns sprang up and choked them." Jesus' explanation is given in verse 22: "Now he who received seed among the thorns is he who hears the word, and the cares of this world and the deceitfulness of riches choke the word, and he becomes unfruitful."

This person has a cluttered mind. He comes to church or Bible study, and while the Word is being delivered, his mind churns with questions: Did I turn the stove off? What am I going to do tomorrow? What can I do to make more sales this week? Will I get a raise this month?

The cluttered mind is full of yesterday, today, and tomorrow, full of things, people, money, business, and school. Tremendous thornbushes of worldly worries suffocate the Word of God. Satan bombards our minds with so many things that there's no room for God anymore. It becomes difficult for God to speak to our hearts when our minds are so cluttered with other things.

Have you ever sat in front of the television, or listened to the radio or a tape, and had your mind on the Word of God? The next thing you knew you were dreaming of your summer vacation. Have you ever come before the Lord for a devotion, and your mind was humming with business or home or children? While those things are natural and normal to think about, Satan will do all he can to detour our minds away from the important task at hand, and that is listening to what God has to say. That is why it is so very important that our hearts be prepared, lest we miss the important truths that God desires to share with us.

The best step to take in this instance is to quickly bring your attention back to God and change gears a bit. If you were praying, turn to Psalms and begin reading. If your eyes and mind became heavy while reading Scripture, close the Bible for a few minutes and consciously praise God.

Praising God through thanksgiving and through acknowledging His character and attributes is one of the best ways I know to break the bonds of a wandering mind. David said that God inhabits the praises of His people (see Ps. 22:3). Praising God brings God warmly near in our hearts. Singing hymns out loud is also a good tool to chase off the devil of diversion.

The most priceless information ever put between two covers is found in the Bible, and there is something wrong in the thinking of a person who will not give concentrated attention for a period of time to hear its magnificent truth.

A COMMITTED MIND

Jesus delineated a fourth type of hearer in verse 8: "But others fell on good ground and yielded a crop: some a hundredfold, some sixty, some thirty." He expounds on that in verse 23: "But he who received seed on the good ground is he who hears the word and understands it, who indeed bears fruit and produced: some a hundredfold, some sixty, some thirty." The committed mind is pictured as fertile soil. It has been cultivated, ready for the seed to penetrate. It can enclose the seed, envelop the seed, provide the heat and moisture needed for the seed to germinate and bring forth fruit. The committed mind is the teachable mind. God can instruct a teachable man or woman in anything. The finest intellect in the world who is not teachable will miss the great truths of God.

A child's mind is a wonderful example of the teachable spirit. Children believe with hearts open and impressionable. They are sensitive, and they want to learn.

Although adults have all sorts of skepticisms, doubts, and hang-ups, certain principles can help cultivate the fertile soil Jesus described. First, we must commit ourselves *to listen carefully to His message* through our pastor, a friend, a book, a television or a radio program, or a Bible-study group.

Second, we must commit ourselves by faith *to resist outside clutter.* When scattered thoughts bombard us, we must purposely refuse to listen and ask the Lord to help us concentrate on His Word. This can only be done by faith in the Lord Jesus Christ because He is the One who enables us to receive the Word clearly.

Third, we must make a commitment *to evaluate our lives* in the light of what we hear. We must take the initiative to sift through the truths we encounter. Fourth, we must make a commitment *to apply the truths that God impresses in our hearts.* If we don't, Satan will steal them quickly. Fifth, we must make a commitment *to obey those truths* that God has impressed upon our lives. When we obey the truths God has impressed on us, we grow into productive fruit-bearing believers. If we don't, we can attend church fifty-two Sundays a year and still be the spiritual babes we were before we began. Preaching and the power of the Word have had no impact upon our lives because we have not obeyed.

It is spiritually impossible to apply the Word week after week and remain the same. As listeners with committed minds, we become productive, maturing children of God.

The fruitful mind-set begins with the seed of a committed mind, blossoming into the productive disciple who hears and obeys God with power and clarity. His garden is fertile.

As the psalmist declared in Psalm 84:5: "Blessed is the man whose strength is in You, Whose heart is set on pilgrimage."

God seeks to support not the closed mind, the cloudy mind, or the cluttered mind but the *committed mind*— the mind of a person "who stands steadfast in his heart" (see 1 Cor. 7:37).

CHAPTER NINE

Hindrances to Hearing

THROUGH THE AGES many sincere Christians have attempted to listen to God. Usually, after several painfully silent sessions, they cease their efforts, claiming that either God doesn't have anything to say to them or they just don't know how to hear Him. We know we have a concerned Father who is more than willing to communicate, and we certainly want to hear from Him. So what's the problem?

I believe that the problem lies on our side, in that we have often accumulated (sometimes unknowingly) spiritual hindrances that prevent us from clearly hearing the Lord.

At least ten contributing factors raise thick barriers to hearing the Voice of God. As we understand what they are, I think it will help us discern why, when we are honestly seeking to perceive what God is saying, we sometimes feel that we might as well be in a spiritually soundproof room, where only our voice reverberates.

1. WE DON'T KNOW GOD

In his book *Knowing God*, J. I. Packer comments:

> We need to frankly face ourselves at this point. We are, perhaps, orthodox evangelicals. We can state the gospel clearly, and can smell unsound doctrine a mile away. If anyone asks us how men may know God we can at once produce the right formula—that we come to know God through Jesus Christ the Lord. Yet the gaiety, goodness and unfetteredness of spirit which are marks of those who have known God are rare among us—rarer, perhaps, than they are to some other Christian circles where, by comparison, evangelical truth is less clearly and fully known. Here, too, it would seem that the last may prove to be first, and the first last. A little knowledge of God is worth more than a great deal of knowledge about Him.

Many believers know Christ as Savior, but they have failed to press on to know His ways and character. If we know Him only as Savior, God cannot speak some things to us because we simply don't know the way He operates. The more we understand who God is, the more we will hear from Him.

That is why it is so urgent that we study the Word of God daily. As we do, we give Him a fertile field in which to work and speak to our hearts. Some Christians know so little about God that they could barely fill up one side of an eight-by-eleven-inch sheet of paper. They have heard lots of conversations, listened to lots of messages, read lots of books, but they simply don't know God personally.

2. A POOR SELF-IMAGE

How many times have we heard people say, "Why would God want to speak to *me*? I am not a preacher or in full-time Christian service. Why in the world would He want to communicate with me?"

The truth is, we are saved, we are sanctified, we are saints, we are children of the living God. Fathers just naturally want to speak to their children; fathers just naturally want their sons or daughters to listen to them. Unfortunately, we often see ourselves in an unworthy light, and when we do, we wonder why a great, magnificent God would speak to us. God could scream in that case, and we could not hear Him.

We must see ourselves as God sees us, that is, as children who need for Him to speak, who need to listen, who need guidance every day of our lives. If we have a pauperlike image of ourselves, wondering why the God who created the heavens and the earth would engage in meaningful conversation with insignificant us, then communication is minimal at best. A beggar taken off the streets of Washington, D. C., would probably have little to say in a personal meeting with the president; but if the president's son were to visit, then a great exchange of pleasant conversation would transpire. It all depends on the relationship. We must remember that we are children of God and that our Father seeks to speak to us.

Psalm 139 is a marvelous comment upon the Father's perfect knowledge of us and His abundant love for us, just the way we are. He knows our frame. He knows our weaknesses. He knows our innermost hurts, fears, and frustrations, yet He longs to gain intimacy with us. It is in these scarred, earthen vessels that Jesus has chosen to put His unmatchable presence. He is at home in these earthly tents. We need not be ill at ease but relax and enjoy His fellowship, knowing He died for us while we

were yet hopeless sinners and He has permanently accepted us into His family (with all our undesirable bag-
gage). We are His—lock, stock, and barrel.

3. A FALSE SENSE OF GUILT

There are two kinds of guilt. One is *true guilt*, that is,
it stems from sin against God; we are responsible for it
and we have to deal with it. The second is *false guilt*,
which Satan places on us; this occurs when the devil ac-
cuses us of not living up to God's standards.

Many people live countless years under such deceptive
guilt. They never feel as if they can quite get God's ac-
ceptance; they think they never quite measure up and
never quite please God; they believe they will never be
all that God wants them to be. These people have a difficult time hearing God, because Satan is always accusing
them, saying, "You think God will speak to *you*? Look
what you have done in the past. Do you think He is going
to overlook that?" Everything they hear is sifted through
a preprogrammed pattern of guilty thinking.

That is the devil's deception because God has forgiven
us, and when we are forgiven, that settles it. Individuals
whose hearts are guilt-ridden are ones whose prayers are
primarily self-centered, because they are so concerned
about what is wrong with themselves and how to get
their act together. When we feel under such condemnation from God, we are almost afraid to listen because we
can't stand any more judgment.

Following an evening service an elderly woman took
my hand in hers, looked me in the eyes, and briefly
shared with me her spiritual pilgrimage. She began by

thanking me for showing her a truth she had missed for fifty-five years of her Christian life. She said that all of her life she had felt unworthy, guilty, and displeasing to God. She had confessed, repented, rededicated her life time after time, but the same old cloud of guilt hovered over her wherever she went.

One Sunday morning she watched our television program *In Touch*. I was preaching a series entitled "How the Truth Can Set You Free," and I explained the difference between true guilt and false guilt. She said, "All of a sudden I saw it. For the first time I understood what God had done with my guilt at the cross." Her eyes sparkled and her face lit up. She said, "That Sunday I was freed of fifty-five long years of a burden God never intended me to bear, for He had borne it all in my behalf two thousand years before on the cross." She was set free at last!

4. BUSINESS/BUSYNESS

It is impossible to live in today's world without being busy. We all have schedules to meet, problems to solve, people to relate to on a continuing basis. So, when I refer to *business* (or busyness), I am not talking about shirking responsibilities on the job or in the home.

If we walk in the Spirit, we have learned to carry out our job and family functions while being able to commune with the heavenly Father. We cannot separate the spiritual and secular because God indwells our lives; He is in the midst of all we do and say. Yet it is easy in the midst of all the clamoring voices of our society to miss the still, small Voice of God. We must be careful to remain sensitive to His presence.

We can come to the end of a hectic day, having walked with Him and abided in His presence, and be perfectly at rest. However, on those days when God seems to be put into a remote corner, we are often weary and strained. Learning to listen to God amid mass confusion is a wonderful strengthener and relaxer.

I used to work in a part of a textile mill that was near a hot bleachery. The temperature was usually over a hundred degrees. I couldn't stand twenty minutes without being absolutely soaked, and all around were the deafening convulsions of machinery. After a week, I learned that was a sweet sound because it drowned out everything but God. I could stand there eight hours a day and talk out loud to God.

Of course, I could have let that rumbling absolutely silence God, but I didn't. Business can be an excuse or a hindrance in hearing God, but it need not be if we learn how to abide in Him.

5. UNBELIEF

Many people do not fully believe that God speaks today. If we think we get direction only through Scripture, then we will miss out on much of what God has to share, because He will speak so often through His Spirit, circumstances, and other people. We must make absolutely certain that we are fully convinced and persuaded that *God does speak to us personally about our families, our businesses, our finances, our hurts, our frustrations, our fears.*

God doesn't speak to just an elite few. We are all in the same category when it comes to His speaking and our listening. He treats all His children on an equal basis.

6. GOD-DIRECTED ANGER

Can you really hear someone else when you are angry, bitter, resentful, and hostile toward him? I don't think so. During my nearly three decades of ministry, I have occasionally met people who are just plain angry toward God.

Perhaps a spouse died, or a child was killed in the prime of life, or the finances collapsed. No matter what the event, they don't understand why God allowed it; so they become angry toward Him. When they pray, they seem to continually recall those bitter moments and express their anger. They want to blame God for their problems. They pray and suddenly discover their hostility gushing forth out of their mouths toward God. He will not retaliate. He understands our anger, but we must recognize that our rage obstructs our spiritual ears. Emotions so out of control make it impossible to receive any words from the Lord.

Such swells of emotion are often a natural response to tragedy, generating huge, crashing waves of hostility toward God or others. I have witnessed many families who have endured these times, yet clung tenaciously to Christ until the raging subsided. Finally, a period of calm came when they could speak to God quietly and regain the joy of hearing His compassionate reply.

7. HARBORING SIN

Harboring a sin is different from *committing* a sin. Harboring a sin means knowing sin is present, knowing

God has put His finger on it, and still not settling it. Harbored sin is like static on the radio. We faintly hear God's Voice, but we can't make it out.

When we have persistently prayed about a problem and God remains silent, we need to look within to check for concealed sin. We may not even be aware we are hiding it. That is why nothing but a close examination will do. When God pins us down on a certain sin, and we say no, I don't know that He will say anything else to us until we obey His original command. Why should God keep speaking to us, if we don't intend to obey? Harbored sin clouds our vision, divides our minds, and plugs our ears.

In one of the churches I pastored, we had a campaign to pay off a rather large debt on which the church was paying a high rate of interest. I chose two church leaders to direct the campaign so that we could settle the debt in a matter of weeks. Those two men had been friends for many years. Both had helped start the church and had been involved in every area of church work.

A decision arose in which they disagreed. When the church voted in one's favor, the other immediately became angry, bitter, and hostile; he stopped attending church and took his family with him. All this resentment was directed toward his best friend!

He refused to listen to any pleas for reconciliation. I watched the heartbreaking consequences of his growing bitterness. Within a year, his business was nearly bankrupt. He suffered a heart attack. He became a recluse. His son rebelled. His wife threatened to leave him. Yet none of these events had an effect on him. Within a few years he died a defeated, broken man. He could not give up his bitterness, his unforgiving spirit.

8. A REBELLIOUS SPIRIT

A rebellious person may want to pray, but he does not want to hear. God will speak to the rebellious heart to repent of a sin, but if no change occurs, God will not speak on other subjects. Rebellion blockades God's penetrating Voice.

Rebellion is not the same as reluctance. God understands our hesitation at times, just as when He spoke with Moses. If you remember, when God called Moses, Moses basically told the Lord that He had the wrong man. After all, he had been feeding sheep for forty years, and God wanted him to go back to Pharaoh and lead over two and a half million people out of Egyptian bondage. We probably would have been reluctant too! Like Moses, we can tell God we don't like what He is saying, but rebellion against His instructions is a different matter.

As a pastor in Florida some years ago, I felt the Lord calling me to Atlanta. The problem was, I didn't want to go. I liked Florida. I liked the beach. There wasn't any traffic, and three or four fishing lakes were one block from my house. So I told the Lord, "Lord, I want to stay where I am." (There is no use trying to hide anything from God, because He knows how we feel anyway.) After working through my initial disinclination, I discovered that Atlanta was exactly where I was supposed to be. I was somewhat indisposed to moving, but I wasn't rebellious. Rebellion tells God that we refuse to do what He wants us to do. God can work with our reluctance by changing our desires, but our rebellion is another matter.

9. REJECTING GOD'S MESSENGERS

Sometimes a husband doesn't want to hear God speak through his wife. Sometimes a wife doesn't want to hear God speak through her husband. They think they are simply turning each other off, when in reality they might be turning God off. When a son or daughter says to the parents, "You love me only when I do what you want me to do," God may be trying to tell those parents they are not loving their children unconditionally the way He loves them.

God will speak to us not only through unwelcomed people but also through objectional circumstances. When God spoke to the apostle Paul on the Damascus Road, the circumstances were less than favorable, because the Spirit of God knocked Paul down and blinded him. Our circumstances, too, may be less than desirable. That doesn't mean that God can't speak through them. Sometimes because of our rebellion against God, He has to get our attention the hard way. I know that God often incapacitates me physically when He wants me to listen. I don't like the circumstances God uses, but I do like the results.

God isn't brutal, but He will do what He has to, to build godly character. We may not like the vessel or situation through which He speaks, but if we listen, it will accomplish His task, and that is the most important thing.

10. UNTRAINED TO LISTEN

Listening to God isn't something we come into the world automatically knowing how to do. We have to *train* ourselves to listen. We are often hindered from hearing God because of our inexperience, but there are some godly tools we can firmly grasp to assist us in hearing from God. He is the quintessential Equipper, supplying us with every necessity for total obedience.

First, we should ask questions. If we are going to listen, we have to learn to be inquisitive. By mentally proposing such questions as, "God, what are You trying to say to me?" we give God the opportunity to reply and reveal His answer. God always has the answers, but it is up to us sometimes to ask the right questions. An inquisitive heart is essential to hearing God.

Second, we should anticipate God's speaking. The Scriptures promise that God will speak, and we should take Him at His Word and be eager to hear Him. The Bible says, "Jesus Christ is the same yesterday, today, and forever" (Heb. 13:8). That means that if God spoke in past history (that is, yesterday), He still speaks today, and He will speak throughout eternity.

Third, we should respond to what we hear. If we make no response to what God says, we will never learn to hear. If we do not positively know that we have heard from God, then we must actively move in the direction we believe God spoke. We learn this way because we take a step of faith. Since God is a loving Father, if He sees us move in the wrong direction, He will correct our course so that we walk in the truth. We may not hear rightly every time, but that is part of the learning process too. How many times does a child fall before he learns to walk? We don't ask him to walk across the room on his first attempt. Some of us are a lot like Samuel: God must speak several times before we finally recognize Him.

Fourth, we should be alert to confirming events. Time after time God confirms His message. He speaks, we obey, and confirmation will quite frequently follow.

Fifth, we should ask God to speak to us. Before you go to bed at night, why don't you tell the Lord that you are listening to Him and that you are available to hear what He has to say anytime during the night? You will be amazed at how many needed solutions to trying problems will almost effortlessly formulate, how deep hurts will soothingly be healed, as you tell God that you are ready and willing to hear His Voice.

As we inquire of God, anticipate His speaking, respond to what we hear, are alert to His confirmations, and simply ask Him to speak clearly, we set the stage for the greatest adventure known to man—hearing Almighty God deliver His message to us. What greater privilege, what greater responsibility could we desire?

CHAPTER TEN

Listening and Obeying

A YOUNG MAN who once came to me was probably as gifted in the ministry as anyone I have ever met. He was extremely well trained and equipped for godly service. He came to me with a decision, and as he began to share, the Spirit of God spoke in my heart with a quick alarm. A red light flashed within, and I said, "Don't do it. You're not ready." I explained to him why and entreated him to listen to me. He wouldn't. He decided he was ready, the time was right, and he turned a deaf ear to what God was trying to say to him. After two years he lost his ministry, his marriage, and everything he owned, including his self-respect. Several years later, I received a letter from him. It began, "Dear Dr. Stanley, If I had only listened!"

I firmly believe God gave this young minister His counsel through the insight the Spirit of God planted in my heart. The young man heard God speak, but he declined to heed God's warning.

As one goes through Scripture, it becomes evident that listening's crucial companion and completing mate is *obedience*. Throughout the Old Testament, God repeatedly exclaimed, "O Israel, you should listen and be careful to do it." It was not that Israel failed to hear God. He sent His servants—Moses, Joshua, Jeremiah, Isaiah, and dozens of others—to His people with clarion announcements. They heard His intentions all right; they just didn't comply. Just as their frequent difficulties stemmed from not obeying God's voice, so, too, does much of the pain, hurt, and suffering in our lives result from failing to respond obediently to God's Voice.

It is significant that in the first couple God created were the features of those who listen but refuse to heed, and so reap the painful harvest of disobedience. Genesis 2:15-17 capsulizes this perennial principle:

> Then the LORD God took the man and put him in the garden of Eden to tend and keep it. And the LORD God commanded the man, saying, "Of every tree of the garden you may freely eat; but of the tree of the knowledge of good and evil you shall not eat, for in the day that you eat of it you shall surely die."

Although Eve did not sin against God until she partook of the fruit, the results of hearing but failing to act appropriately are clearly demonstrated in her life. God had placed in the Garden of Eden a perfect environment. Adam and Eve and everything in it were heavenly. His instructions to maintain this pristine life were as lucid as a cloudless sky. "It's all yours. I created this for you. It's available to you for your enjoyment and your pleasure. All I want you to do is take care of it. I will give you the strength and wisdom to do so." Then He added, "I have only one restriction. There is one tree in this garden that I have put a circle around, and under no condition are you to eat of the fruit of the tree of the knowledge of good and evil. For the day that you eat that fruit, you shall surely die."

There was no way for Adam and Eve to mistake what God said. He was very clear, concise, and brief. They could not forget that simple word of caution and admonition. Isn't it strange, when we think about our own lives and God's provision, how Satan points to the one thing we have no business doing? Isn't it amazing how he enlarges the one forbidden area? Every "thou shalt not" in the Bible is a promise of God's protection; He always looks out for our best interests. He is not preventing us from enjoying life, rather he is preventing us from destroying ourselves and placing ourselves in a position where we cannot enjoy life. Every "thou shalt not" is an expression of divine love to His children.

Of course, we know that Satan tempted Adam and Eve. Eve ate the fruit, offered Adam a bite, and sin entered the world, so that we still suffer the result of their indiscretion. I want to share eight principles based on this scriptural account which soberly depict what happens when we fail to hear God's revelation. They are enduring truths which know no boundaries as to season, age, or era.

WE LISTEN TO THE WRONG VOICES

First, when we fail to listen to God, we listen to the wrong voices. Unlike Eve, we do not live in the Garden of Eden where there is no sin. We live in a world rampant with sin, and when we turn deaf ears to what we know God is saying, we listen to the wrong voices. We begin to pay attention to other attractive voices that have only one thing in mind—our ultimate destruction. One of the most tragic acts anyone can carry out is to turn a deaf ear to almighty God. Thus, Satan is given a place instead. We often know what God wants us to do, but somehow we say, "I know, Lord, but—" When we say *but*, we're really telling the Lord we don't want to hear what He is saying. It is then we turn our ears to those voices that lead us away from the will of God, away from His purpose in our lives.

WE ARE EASILY DECEIVED

Second, when we fail to listen to God, we are easily deceived. Genesis 3:1–4 records Satan's conversation with Eve:

> Now the serpent was more cunning than any beast of the field which the LORD God had made. And he said to the woman, "Has God indeed said, 'You shall not eat of every tree of the garden'?" And the woman said to the serpent, "We may eat the fruit of the trees of the garden; but of the fruit of the tree which is in the midst of the garden, God has said, 'You shall not eat it, nor shall you touch it, lest you die.' " And the serpent said to the woman, "You will not surely die."

That is, he said, "Now look, let's get the full viewpoint of this thing. I know what God said, but let's not get so narrow-minded about this. The truth is, you surely shall not die."

Friends, when we listen to other voices, we become easily deceived. Satan, who is the father of all lies, deceived Eve by his cunning, crafty, subtle words. (He used almost the same words God used.) Not choosing to listen to God when we know He is speaking to us is an act of rebellion. When we listen to voices other than God's Voice, our perspective becomes unbalanced. The individual who is tuned in to God and who listens to God is mentally sharper and clearer than the person who does not listen to God when it comes to spiritual or moral issues. He has a perception, an awareness, an attentiveness that others do not possess. There is a power to concentrate, a discernment that the nonlistener does not have.

Satan easily deceives us by saying, "You don't mean to tell me that you think you're going to be like your parents? Your parents grew up in a whole different generation. They went to church because there wasn't anything else to do. They didn't have television and all the activities that are happening. Going to church Sunday morning, Sunday night, and Wednesday night was their entertainment. This is a whole different age, a whole different society. Surely, you don't want to be like them!"

Whenever we get in a conversation with the devil, we are headed for failure. His appeal is to our flesh. The more we listen, the less distinct God's Voice becomes. Satan's shouts all too easily deafen our ears to God's still, small Voice. We find ourselves thinking illogical thoughts, rationalizing, and tolerating attitudes and actions that we know are wrong. When we fail to listen to Him, the other voices sound so inviting.

WE EXPRESS PRIDE AND INDEPENDENCE OF GOD

Third, when we fail to listen to God, we express pride and independence of God. The bottom line of all sin is *independence.* Satan told Eve, "For God knows that in the day you eat of it your eyes will be opened, and you will be like God, knowing good and evil" (Gen. 3:5). What he did *not* tell her was, "Eve, you're going to be like God, knowing good and evil, but I'm here to tell you Eve, you're going to hate the day you ever learned the truth about evil."

Every single time we choose to disobey God's revealed truth, we choose to act independently of Him. It is an expression of our pride. We tell God we can handle it. We declare to an omniscient God (who knows our past, present, and future) that we're making the best choice. That's like a five year old dictating the menu to his mother because he knows what is most nourishing. Isn't that foolish? Isn't that the epitome of all folly, that we would act independently of God because we think we know what's best right now? We'll never know better than God knows. Just as Satan slyly conned Eve into subtle pride, so he lures many young people into sin because their friends say, "Well, you'll never know till you try it."

Wouldn't each of us agree that we have learned some things in life we wish we had never learned? We've experienced what we wish we had never experienced? That's the subtlety. When we fail to listen to Him, we listen to other voices whose appeal is that of independence and pride, and whose value system is the antithesis of God's.

WE MAKE DECISIONS THAT APPEAL TO THE FLESH

Fourth, when we fail to listen to God, we make decisions that appeal to the flesh, not to the spirit. Satan doesn't appeal to us concerning our hunger for God. He doesn't appeal to us concerning our thirst to know Him. He doesn't appeal to us in our desire to be obedient to God. He doesn't appeal to us in our desire to know the Word of God. He doesn't appeal to us in our desire to understand the meaning of prevailing prayer. What does he appeal to?

What did he appeal to, to Eve? Genesis 3:6 explains: "So when the woman saw that the tree was good for food, that it was pleasant to the eyes, and a tree desirable to make one wise, she took of its fruit and ate. She also gave to her husband with her, and he ate." Satan appealed to Eve's desire for wisdom to make her eat from the tree.

On the other hand, God is interested in speaking to our spirits. He is interested in what is best for us and our families. Even though we have been saved and have a brand-new nature, the principle of sin abides within us. We no longer have to yield to it or be dominated by it—unless we choose to be. We are no longer conquered by it—unless we give in to it. There is a power working within us greater than all the power of sin, Satan, and hell.

But when we cease to listen to God, we listen to what appeals to the flesh, and so we are deceived. Our names may be written in the Lamb's Book of Life, but if we don't listen to God, the same Satan who appeals to the unbeliever will use the same methods to appeal to us as believers.

That's why we must be people of God whose ears are bent to listening to God. The world speaks a different language from the one God speaks. The world marches to a different drumbeat from the one God marches to. God wants our ears tuned to Him because He wants to give us divine directions and because He has our best interests at heart. If we are honest today, however, we'll have to admit, whenever we stop listening to Him, we start listening and making decisions based on things that appeal to the flesh, not the spirit.

WE MAKE EXCUSES FOR OUR WRONGS

Fifth, when we fail to listen to God, we make excuses for our wrongs. Genesis 3:8-9 says that when the Lord God came walking in the garden in the cool of the day,

"Adam and his wife hid themselves from the presence of the LORD God among the trees of the garden. Then the LORD God called to Adam and said to him, 'Where are you'?"

Don't think for a minute that God didn't know where Adam was. He wasn't asking for information. He knew exactly where Adam and Eve were, physically, emotionally, spiritually, and mentally. Adam responded: "I heard Your voice in the garden, and I was afraid because I was naked; and I hid myself" (Gen. 3:10). Remember, Adam had never been afraid before. Fear was a brand-new emotional experience. He was hiding out of fear, just as many of us hide emotionally and spiritually.

God said: "Who told you that you were naked? Have you eaten from the tree of which I commanded you that you should not eat?" (Gen. 3:11). God never asks questions to find out information. God asks questions to receive a confession; so He queried Adam. Adam's tragic reply is found in Genesis 3:12: "The woman whom You gave to be with me, she gave me of the tree, and I ate." (He was blaming it on someone else.) Listen to the next verse: "And the LORD God said to the woman, 'What is this you have done?' And the woman said, 'The serpent deceived me, and I ate' " (Gen. 3:13).

You know what? That's what we do today. God speaks to us, and we know exactly what He is saying. We try to rationalize our disobedience, but God doesn't listen to any excuses. When God speaks and we turn a deaf ear, our alibis are unacceptable. We can't blame somebody else.

God had spoken very concisely to Adam who told Eve. Eve couldn't tell God, "I couldn't remember Your instructions," because God had said clearly, "Of every tree of the garden you may freely eat; but of the tree of the knowledge of good and evil you shall not eat, for in the day that you eat of it you shall surely die" (Gen. 2:16–17). That is the point!

Since God knows our future, our personalities, and our capacity to listen, He isn't ever going to say more to us than we can deal with at the moment. So we can't blame our failures to listen on anyone else. I've come to the Lord on many occasions and tried to plea bargain away some of my inadequacies. I rationalized some of my behavior, blaming it on the death of my father when I was very young. Then one day God showed me that I couldn't blame my sin and pain on any person or circumstance. It makes no difference what happened to me or you. I'm responsible for my responses, and you are responsible for yours.

WE WILL SUFFER THE CONSEQUENCES

Sixth, when we fail to listen to God, we will suffer the consequences. When God finished talking with Adam and Eve, He listed the consequences that both Satan and they would have to endure. Genesis 3:14–15 indicts Satan:

> So the LORD God said to the serpent:
>
> "Because you have done this,
>   You are cursed more than all cattle,
>   And more than every beast of the field;
> On your belly you shall go,
>   And you shall eat dust
>   All the days of your life.
> And I will put enmity
>   Between you and the woman,
>   And between your seed and her Seed;

He [Christ] shall bruise your [Satan's] head,
And you shall bruise His heel" [that's the Cross].

Satan did injure Him because of sin, but Jesus Christ the eternal Son of God was the Victor. Then in verses 16–19, God listed the painful results of Adam and Eve's rebellion:

To the woman He said:

"I will greatly multiply
    your sorrow and your conception;
In pain you shall bring forth children;
Your desire shall be for your husband,
And he shall rule over you."

Then to Adam He said, "Because you have heeded the voice of your wife, and have eaten from the tree of which I commanded you, saying, 'You shall not eat of it':

"Cursed is the ground for your sake;
In toil you shall eat of it
All the days of your life.
Both thorns and thistles
    it shall bring forth for you,
And you shall eat the herb of the field.
In the sweat of your face
    you shall eat bread
Till you return to the ground,
For out of it you were taken;
For dust you are,
And to dust you shall return."

Later, the Bible says He cast them out of the garden (Gen. 3:23–24). When Adam and Eve ceased to listen to God but listened to another voice, they lost it all and suffering began. All suffering and pain ultimately can be traced to the evil of the garden.

When we fail to listen, we will suffer the consequences. The most serious business today that you and I should engage in is listening and heeding the Voice of

God. As a pastor, I have seen much suffering because people refused to obey God's counsel. One particularly successful minister wanted to enter a new field of ministry. Some very professional people advised him that he was not capable of engaging in that work. Everyone who knew him and loved him, everyone who was looking out for his best interests, said, "Please don't." He turned a deaf ear to this wise, godly counsel. It cost him his life.

How many times have I sat down with a distraught father who had counseled his daughter, "Honey, don't, don't, don't go out with that fellow. There's something about him that tells me you should avoid him. He doesn't have a godly mind." She turned down God's Voice through her father, and ended up pregnant, ruining her life.

So many pregnant teenagers have listened to the deceiving voices of evil and now have to live with tons of guilt that only God will be able to remove.

Literally dozens of men I have known have confessed, "If I had only listened to my wife. She told me it was a bad deal, but I figured she didn't know anything about money or finances. She pleaded with me not to go through with it. I wouldn't listen, and I lost it all!"

During one marriage counseling session, I said to the young woman seated beside her fiance, "Don't marry this man; he doesn't love you." They both looked strangely at me. I explained, "Let me tell you why he doesn't love you. When I asked him these crucial questions concerning the values of the marriage relationship, he gave me the wrong answers to every one. There is no evidence of his love for you but only evidence of his desire for gratification of the flesh." She didn't listen. Someone else married them because I wouldn't perform the ceremony. I can still remember her, standing in my office door one day, tears streaming down her cheeks. It had only been four months since their marriage, and she said, "If I'd only listened to you...." There is no way to turn a deaf ear to God without suffering.

After a church service a few years ago, a young woman came up to me and related this story: "I know exactly what you were talking about this morning. I knew when I married my husband, who was an alcoholic and not a Christian, I shouldn't have done it. I knew that wasn't what God wanted me to do. But I did, and my marriage is wrecked, lost, and gone forever. God is just now beginning to put the pieces of my life back together."

Before you get ready to do something, if there is a gnawing deep inside, a sneaking suspicion, think twice before acting, because God could be telling you, "No!" Be wise enough to stop, confront God, and say, "Lord, would You tell me one more time what Your will is in this matter?" God will tell you the truth and save you a lot of pain.

OTHERS AROUND US ARE HURT

Seven, when we fail to listen to God, others around us are hurt. You cannot sin in isolation. When a husband fails to listen to God, his wife hurts. When children fail to listen to God, their parents hurt. When a man in business fails to listen to his godly partner, their business hurts. When the leaders of a nation fail to listen to God, everybody in the nation hurts. Other people hurt when we fail to listen.

Adam and Eve's disobedience resulted in the alienation of the entire human race. Their sin in the garden reached around the world.

WE MISS GOD'S VERY BEST

Finally, when we fail to listen to God, we miss His very best. The Garden of Eden was God's best, but Adam and Eve lost it all. My friend, let me ask you a question. Many people are on the brink of losing God's best because they have chosen to listen to a voice other than God's. God has provided the finest for you. If you fail to listen, you'll go through life having missed God's very best. Are you willing to substitute what Satan has to offer you for God's supreme gifts? When you listen and obey, God's best will be yours.

In 1 Samuel 15, Samuel sent Saul on a mission to "Go and attack Amalek, and utterly destroy all that they have, and do not spare them" (v. 3). Saul, however, saved some of the best spoils and spared the king's life. When Samuel discovered Saul's disobedience, Saul replied: "I have sinned, for I have transgressed the commandment of the LORD and your words, because I feared the people and obeyed their voice" (v. 24). Trying to accommodate his fellow warriors and their greed caused Saul to lose his perspective of God's original command to eradicate Amalek and its king.

CHAPTER ELEVEN

The Life That Listens—
A Well-Built Life

USUALLY, WHEN JESUS told a parable, He explained in detail exactly what He meant, even to His apostles. But, the short, penetrating parable in Matthew 7:24–27 is one that needs no clarification. Concluding His dramatic sermon, Jesus drove home this inescapable truth:

> Therefore whoever hears these sayings of Mine, and does them, I will liken him to a wise man who built his house on the rock: and the rain descended, the floods came, and the winds blew and beat on that house; and it did not fall, for it was founded on the rock. Now everyone who hears these sayings of Mine, and does not do them, will be like a foolish man who built his house on the sand: and the rain descended, the floods came, and the winds blew and beat on that house; and it fell. And great was its fall.

In this particular parable, Jesus confronts us with the simple truth that each of us is building a life, and its soundness is based on hearing His Voice and acting on it. Jesus wanted the multitudes who had gathered on the rocky hillside to understand that He wasn't delivering just a marvelous new pattern for living. It wasn't to be such a popular sermon that they all went home saying, "Boy, wasn't that a great message!" and then they gradually forgot about it. What He uttered was not meant to be new spiritual fodder for debate in the synagogues or marketplace. He stated *divine truth* to be immediately implemented in every sector of existence.

Verse 29 says, "He taught them as one having authority." It was as though he had said, "Men, women, and children, you have just heard My words, which come from God. You have listened to My instructions concerning how to be blessed, how to forgive, and how to pray. You have heard great truths about My kingdom and its principles. I leave you now with this final command: Put these truths into practice, and your life will be like the man whose house was constructed on a solid foundation. Ignore, forget, or shelve these truths, and your life will be erected on worthless, porous sand. The choice is yours."

Listening to God and obeying Him are the only constructive methods that enable us to survive the storms of the twentieth century. Hearing His Voice and integrating it into our value systems, behavioral patterns, thoughts, and conversations are the prerequisites for enduring lives. Staying alert and responsive to His speaking Voice becomes the rock foundation that no tempest, temptation, or trial can erode. That's why it's dangerous to attend church, listen to religious broadcasts, or read Christian publications! It's dangerous because Jesus said everyone who hears His truth and does not act upon it will be like the foolish man who built his house upon the sand. It's perilous, because each of us will be held accountable for acting upon every spiritual truth we hear. When the storms come, our conformity to this principle will become evident. Have we built well, hearing God's word and daily applying it, or have we built poorly, hearing but not implementing?

Some people appear successfully established in life, when in reality, they aren't. The external facade may appear sound, but inwardly, they are on the verge of collapse. They may deceive us, but when the final great eternal storm of judgment hits, they will crumble. They can't fool God. Notice verse 24 for a moment. In the English it says, "Therefore whoever hears these sayings of Mine, and does them." The original Greek for Matthew 7:24 reads: "therefore." Why? Because Jesus didn't want anybody to think he was an exception. He emphasized individual responsibility. No one escapes.

THE REQUIREMENTS FOR A WELL-BUILT LIFE

How do we build well-built lives? Jesus gives us two very simple requirements: first, we must hear the Word of God; second, we must obey the Word of God we have encountered. Many Scriptures stress the necessity of first hearing God's Word. Second Timothy 3:16–17 says: "All Scripture is given by inspiration of God, and is profitable for doctrine, for reproof, for correction, for instruction in righteousness, that the man of God may be complete, thoroughly equipped for every good work."

The purpose of Scripture is to build its principles into our lives. Psalm 19:7–8 declares: "The law of the LORD [speaking of the Word] is perfect, converting the soul; The testimony of the LORD is sure, making wise the simple; The statutes of the LORD are right, rejoicing the heart."

Joshua 1:7–8 admonishes:

Only be strong and very courageous, that you may observe to do according to all the law which Moses My servant commanded you; do not turn from it to the right hand
or to the left, that you may prosper wherever you go. This
Book of the Law shall not depart from your mouth, but
you shall meditate in it day and night, that you may observe to do according to all that is written in it. For then
you will make your way prosperous, and then you will
have good success.

The enduring life builds into it the Word of God by giving careful attention to the principles of Scripture, realizing the inevitable consequences. In Colossians 3:16 Paul
amplified the concept: "Let the word of Christ dwell in
you richly in all wisdom, teaching and admonishing one
another in psalms and hymns and spiritual songs, singing
with grace in your hearts to the Lord." Is a person rich
who has one hundred dollars in his bank account and
owes nothing? No. Is a person rich who knows John 3:16
and Psalm 23? Not really, because the Word of God is to
richly dwell in us, overflowing and abounding in our
lives.

The important thing is that we build God's Word into
our lives. I often think about the little children who are
in church when I preach. I know the pictures they draw
are more important to them than the sermon, yet into
these precious, innocent ears the Word of God is making
its impression. Sometimes they don't even understand
it. But it's there, and one day God will resurrect a truth
when they need it the most, given by the Spirit of God.
The frequently unconscious pouring of spiritual truths
and principles sets the foundation of their lives. Then
when the winds begin to blow in their teenage years,
their lives will endure. The principles are there; the
house was built well early in life.

The second requirement for a well-built life is heeding; that is, obeying, making application. These scriptural principles are to direct and govern our lives. Several verses from Psalm 119 help us to understand the importance of obeying God's Word.

> Blessed are the undefiled in the way,
> Who walk in [not just listen, but walk] in the law of
> the LORD.
> Blessed are those who keep His
> testimonies,
> Who seek Him with the whole heart! (vv. 1–2).

> Your testimonies also are my delight
> And my counselors (v. 24).

> Teach me, O LORD, the way of Your
> statutes,
> And I shall keep it to the end.
> Give me understanding,
> and I shall keep Your law;
> Indeed, I shall observe it with my
> whole heart (vv. 33–34).

> It is good for me that I have been
> afflicted,
> That I may learn Your statutes [because he says as a
> result of learning those statutes, his values have changed].
> [Now] The law of Your mouth [the Word of God] is bet-
> ter to me
> Than thousands of coins of gold and
> silver (vv. 71–72).

> Great peace have those who love
> Your law,
> And nothing causes them to stumble (v. 165).

The blessings, peace, and wisdom were results of applying Scripture and learning that God is faithful to His Word. In chapter 11 of Luke, Jesus said something most significant. "And it happened, as He spoke these things, that a certain woman from the crowd raised her voice and said to Him, 'Blessed is the womb that bore You, and the breasts which nursed You!' " (v. 27). Jesus' response in verse 28 revealed the composition of His family! He said, "More than that, blessed are those who hear the word of God and keep it!" Jesus was saying more blessed than Mary who gave birth to Me is the one who hears the Word of God and makes application.

The wise man or woman will listen intently to the principles of Scripture and having heard them, will act upon them, will apply them in life, and will be directed by the principles of truth. Jesus said a foolish person isn't one who hears, but one who hears and doesn't act. In the parable both heard: one acted on what he heard and one ignored it. There are only two categories. The ones who act upon truth received—build upon the rock; the ones who fail to act—build upon the sand. While knowing the requirements for the well-built life is essential, perceiving the reasons for such spiritual construction is no less vital.

THE REASONS FOR A WELL-BUILT LIFE

Someone once described the Christian life as "heading into a storm, being in a storm, or coming out of a storm." Thus, the first reason for a well-built life is that regardless of frequency, *storms are inevitable.* They are going to come. Jesus didn't say, "*If* it rains"; "*If* there are floods"; "*If* the winds blow." He said, "and the rain descended, and the floods came, and the winds blew."

There are unavoidable storms that come into our marriages, our finances; storms that rain down upon us with disappointment; storms that flood us with physical illness and disease. They come into every aspect of life, but they do come. It doesn't make any difference whether we've built upon the rock or upon the sand, the storms are coming to us all. The winds will blow upon those lives built upon the rock *and* the sand. Torrential rains deluge both kinds of builders. It isn't a matter of whether or not we're going to have storms in our lives. The question is, how are we building our lives, and will we survive and endure the storms when they do come?

Storms don't wait until we reach sixty years of age—they'll hit us young; they'll hit us in middle age; they'll hit us in later years. They will come at all stages of our lives!

Storms are not just inevitable; they are uncontrollable. We can't control torrential rainstorms coming down in sheets. We can't harness floods. On television several times a year, we see houses washing away, buildings crumbling, mountainsides shifting because of floods. We can't control the blowing of the wind. Jesus said to Nicodemus, "The wind blows where it wishes, and you hear the sound of it, but cannot tell where it comes from and where it goes" (John 3:8). We face many situations and circumstances over which we have no control. Somebody else makes the decision; something happens that's totally beyond our control. How our lives have been built will determine whether we crumble or hold fast.

When we build our houses we should consider not only the inevitability of storms but also the indestructibility of a well-built house. When we think about a well-built life, we have to think first in terms of the foundation, which is the eternal rock of Jesus Christ. In 1 Corinthians 10, Paul, referring to those Old Testament saints coming out of Egyptian bondage and passing through the Red Sea, said, "And all drank the same spiritual drink.

For they drank of that spiritual Rock that followed them, and that Rock was Christ" (v. 4). He simply identified the rock as Jesus Christ. We sing, "My hope is built on nothing less/Than Jesus' blood and righteousness"; "On Christ, the solid rock, I stand;/All other ground is sinking sand." When we received Jesus Christ as our personal Savior, God founded us upon the Rock, the immovable, eternal Rock.

Second, a well-built life is comprised of lasting, enduring substance. The Bible says in Isaiah 40:8, "The grass withers, the flower fades, But the word of our God stands forever." The substance of God's Word is our imperishable building material. God intends for us to build our lives on the principles of Scripture. We should be governed, dominated, undergirded, and directed by the principles of Scripture. The living Word of God should prevail in every aspect of our lives. The well-built life is fashioned of substance that is eternal, because we are not just physical beings but also spiritual beings. Therefore, the substance of our lives must be spiritual.

Every day our thoughts and our actions build a life for good or for bad. To last, we must build upon the eternal Rock, built with the eternal substance of the Word of God for an eternal home. Jesus told us in John 14:2–3, "In My Father's house are many mansions; if it were not so, I would have told you. I go to prepare a place for you. And if I go and prepare a place for you, I will come again and receive you to Myself; that where I am, there you may be also." We are building for an eternal home; our lives are built for an eternal purpose.

In Ephesians 2:6–7 Paul said, "And raised us up together, and made us sit together in the heavenly places in Christ Jesus, that in the ages to come He might show the exceeding riches of His grace in His kindness toward us in Christ Jesus." God saved us so that for all of eternity He can parade us in heaven, portraying the matchless grace He bestowed upon us when we were undeserving sinners. We are the trophies of the Lord Jesus Christ. We are building lives with an eternal purpose in mind, which is to glorify, radiate, and reflect God forever. That construction is a present-day endeavor.

We are building into our lives now the degree to which we will glorify God. First Corinthians 10:15 revealed that our earthly lives are building projects that determine our heavenly rewards. One of the most foolish things a person can say is, "I will live the way I choose to live today. I will change tomorrow, and then I will give the rest of my life to God." The young person who says, "I'm going to enjoy life now; later on, I'll give it to God," falls headlong into the devil's snare. Satan knows life's foundation must be right.

The storms are inevitable, they are unavoidable, they are coming. But when we build our lives upon the eternal Rock, out of eternal substance, for an eternal home, with an eternal purpose in mind, for eternal living, the Bible says we are "wise men" (Matt. 7:24).

A third reason to build our houses well is to avoid the inescapable consequences of poorly built houses. Jesus said the one who decided to build his house upon the sand lost everything when the storms hit. The same rains, floods, and winds that struck the house on the rock struck him, but his house collapsed. The life that is poorly built leaves Christ out and makes no application of the Word of God. This is the life of a man who hears the Word of God and ignores it, rejects it, and refuses it. That is why it is dangerous to come to church. It would be hard to measure how much truth has entered our ears in our lifetimes. What is more important, however, is how much of that truth we have acted upon. Jesus couldn't have said it any simpler. He said, if we are smart, we will listen aggressively to the Word of God and will act upon what we hear. If we want to play the fool, we will hear the Voice of God and ignore it, reject it, or try to forget it. But when the storm hits us from all sides, coming down like rain from above, rising around us like a flood, flowing all about us, then we will be glad we have built lives that listen to God and obey Him. We will survive and endure the greatest storms of life.

THE REWARDS OF A WELL-BUILT LIFE

What are the rewards of a well-built life? *First, we endure the storms.* Financial, marital, or whatever they may be, we can endure them. *Second, we have the capacity to enjoy the pleasures of life.* The person who has built his house upon the Rock and has built his life out of the substance of God's Word has a peace that sustains him through difficulties, heartaches, and trials. He has the capacity to enjoy the pleasures of life, and he knows the pleasures are genuine. Some things the world offers as pleasure bring only pain. He can discern what is good for him and what is not; what has lasting value and what does not; and what brings true pleasure and what does not.

Third, a life that is well built will enrich the lives of others. When we build into our lives the substance of the Word of God, that will overflow into the lives of people we meet. We become change points in their lives. They meet us and their lives change. They want what we want. They want to discover what we have discovered. Each of us who is richly endowed by the Word of God has something eternal to offer every single person we meet.

The fourth reward of a well-built life is continuing spiritual growth. What if the storms come? When the storm is over, we can praise God for His faithfulness again. We discover more and more about who He is. The tremendous blessings of God pour into our lives when we are faithful to Him in the storms. When we are faithful to God, listening to His voice and obeying it, He will honor and bless us.

CONCLUSION

Elijah was one of the mightiest prophets of the Old Testament. His miraculous ministry had a tremendous impact upon the nation of Israel. He confronted kings, raised the dead, and boldly encountered and destroyed an array of false prophets. Yet, James wrote that he was a "man with a nature like ours" (5:17). As such, he experienced times of great discouragement, evidenced clearly in his flight from Queen Jezebel following his convincing victory over the prophets of Baal.

First Kings 19:4 relates that he went into the wilderness requesting that he "might die." Succored by an angel, he was able to journey "forty days and forty nights as far as Horeb, the mountain of God" (v. 8).

The fact that Elijah traveled for almost six weeks to Mount Horeb (remember he had just recently collapsed in exhaustion) was no accident; Horeb is another name for the majestic Mount Sinai.

At Mount Horeb Moses first saw God in the midst of the burning bush and heard Him speak (see Exod. 3:4); at

Mount Horeb "the LORD came down...on the top of the mountain. And the LORD called Moses to the top of the mountain, and Moses went up" (Exod. 19:20). At Mount Horeb "the glory of the LORD rested...and the cloud covered it six days. And on the seventh day He called to Moses from the midst of the cloud" (Exod. 24:16). At Mount Horeb God instructed Moses to strike the rock and water gushed forth (see Exod 17:6).

Elijah went to Mount Horeb because he knew that was where he could hear God speak. At this point in his ministry, there was nothing he needed more than to hear decisively the comforting Voice of God. No miracle would do. No fellow prophet would suffice. Elijah desperately wanted to hear God.

He was not disappointed. A great wind, earthquake, and fire passed in front of Elijah, but there was no speaking voice. Then suddenly, a quiet breeze stirred at the mouth of Elijah's cave. Immediately he knew he was in the presence of the divine, and he concealed his face in a mantle (much as Moses did when God spoke from the burning bush). In a few brief seconds, God revived the sagging prophet, revealing the future of his ministry, including the imminent recruitment of his successor Elisha who would ensure that Elijah's work would continue (see 1 Kings 19:11–17).

So it is that we, as believers, often weary and worried, need to hear just one thing to refresh, encourage, and strengthen us in our service of the King—*God's voice.* Whatever our situation may call for—guidance, comfort, assurance, strength, perseverance, faith, joy, peace— God's Voice will supply.

The answer will not be found in the noise and rumble (earthquake, wind, and fire) of the world or religion. It is seldom that we will hear accurately from God in the rush of traffic, the din of the office, or the clatter of friends. God wishes to speak to us individually, and for that we must be committed to seek solitude, however brief.

How many times have we waited in line to hear a particularly noted orator speak of religion or politics or sports? How often have we patiently waited in front of a television to tune into the "important news of the day" (apartment fires and floods) or stayed glued to the radio for changes in the weather? How many (literally) thousands of hours have we invested in listening to things that make no eternal difference?

Only a few minutes of sitting before the God who speaks can transform a life, metamorphose a mind, and reset purpose and direction for eternity. The sad heart is cheered, the confused mind is ordered, the pessimistic outlook is eliminated, the lonely spirit is befriended, the rebellious will is subdued, and the drifting seeker is made steadfast.

Wherever Jesus went and taught, He said, "He who has ears let him hear." To those who heard, He called "blessed." To those who rejected His truth, He condemned to further unbelief.

Two thousand years later, we are equipped with everything necessary to confidently hear from God. We are the repositories of the Holy Spirit, who teaches us all things and brings to our remembrance everything Jesus said. We have at our fingertips His completed Word, which is the magnificent sum of God's character, nature, truth, and principles. In a nation that abounds with sincere believers, we have unhindered access to the wise counsel of people who know and love God.

Therefore, we can go "boldly to the throne of grace,

that we may obtain mercy and find grace" (Heb. 4:16). What could be a fuller, richer expression of such grace and mercy than our Father's clear communication to His children?

Laying aside our fears, we can come expectantly, not to a mountain consumed by fire (Mount Horeb) but "to Mount Zion and to the city of the living God" (Heb. 12:22) where He delights to instruct and encourage His people. We will never be disappointed, even if reproof or admonishment is given, for everything God speaks is for our welfare.

Like Mary, we should learn to listen to the Lord's word, seated at His feet (see Luke 10:39). Through quiet, disciplined prayer and interaction with His Word and people, we can become men and women who fruitfully learn to distinguish the speaking Voice from amid the clamor of our environs.

When we do, we too can trust and we have "chosen that good part, which will not be taken away" (Luke 10:42). For when once we have heard God speak, nothing else compares. Everything else pales beside the priceless experience of hearing God. Above all, absolutely nothing—no trouble, no tribulation, no circumstance, no uncertainty—can displace the wonderful peace and assurance that result from definitely being on the receiving end of God's communication.

The man who has heard from God has the enduring power to engage adversaries, confront tragedy, and surmount any problem that lies in his path, because upon what God has spoken, he can steadfastly rest. God fulfills His promises and guarantees His Word.

God is still speaking. Let us choose the "good part" of listening obediently to Him. He has great and mighty things in store for each of us.